Looking Within

Discover 7 Principles Leading to Hope, Peace, and Joy

Pat Heydlauff

Looking Within: Discover 7 Principles Leading to Hope, Peace, and Joy
Copyright © 2022 by Pat Heydlauff

All rights reserved. No part of this book may be used or reproduced by any means, graphic, electronic, or mechanical, including photocopying, recording, taping, or by any information system without the written permission of the publisher, except in the case of brief quotations embodied in critical articles and reviews.

All poems and epigraphs are the original work of Pat Heydlauff unless otherwise noted.

Cover art: "Finding Home," by Pat Heydlauff, ©2020
https://fineartamerica.com/profiles/pat-heydlauff/shop

ISBN: 978-0-9983347-6-9
Published by: Energy Design

Other Books by Pat Heydlauff
Feng Shui So Easy a Child Can Do It
Selling Your Home with a Competitive Edge
21 Ways…to Increase Employee Engagement
The Way We Go: Your Roadmap to a Better Future

Dedication

To everyone seeking to create a world filled with harmony, love, light, and enlightenment

And

To our children, grandchildren, and great-grandchildren who will inherit the world we create

Acknowledgements

The world is a better place when you are directly connected to your Creator, God, the Divine. I am humbly honored and thank God, my Creator, the One for my eternal connection and for putting this message in my heart to share with humanity.

Additionally, I'd like to acknowledge all of my spirit guides, sages, teachers, and my crossed over dearest Grandmother for their guidance, counsel, and wisdom, and for being at my side throughout my journey. Serving along with them has been my spiritual Board of Directors consisting of DaVinci, Rembrandt, Einstein, Gandhi, Thoth, Billy Graham, Black Eagle Feather, and Johann Strauss. They often chime in very vocally with their messages of hope, peace, and encouragement, and they have enriched my life with creativity, knowledge, wisdom, spirituality, and joy. I can often feel the beat of a Strauss waltz in my heart and hear it while writing.

A special acknowledgement goes to hundreds of authors, teachers, and masters that have come before spreading their knowledge of ancient wisdom, eastern and western philosophies, Native American and indigenous cultures' spirituality. Without their many centuries of labor throughout the millennia, this book would have been impossible to write.

I wish to also express my deep appreciation for my family, Lorna West and Ben Heydlauff, who has been there for me in so many ways. They bring a ray of sunshine into my world, even on the darkest of days. I want to also include in this category my friend and spiritual counselor, Monet Brooks, who has helped me find steps on my spiritual journey that lead me to greater clarity and expanded my horizons. Susan Wallace, a friend, a great listener, and astrology sage, has provided me much needed balance, often challenging viewpoints, and at times has dramatically expanded my thinking. Zora Olsson, a longtime dear friend, a beautiful artist, and leader with great panache and style, has always encouraged me whether in our mutually shared field of fine art or in my writing. She always made me feel like I could accomplish anything, including this book. Dawn Josephson, a true wordsmith, has been a different type of sage who poured over my writing and poems, making sure the words spoke my truth, meant what I said, and said what I meant.

And of course, I want to extend a special thank you to YOU, the reader. I value your time for reading my book and am hopeful it will move you to discover your spiritual journey and purpose, find joy in being an active participant in bringing light to a world in need, and give birth to the Renaissance of Joy. May this enrich your life and provide you a better tomorrow filled with hope, peace, prosperity, and joy.

Contents

Introduction 9

Part I: The Great Transformation 17

Chapter 1: Tomorrow is Worth the Wait! 21

Chapter 2: Why Change Must Happen 33

Chapter 3: The Roadmap to the Future 49

Chapter 4: All Divine Paths Lead Home 65

Part II: The Seven Principles of Universal Truth 83

Chapter 5: The First Principle - Wisdom: 85

Chapter 6: The Second Principle - Respect 101

Chapter 7: The Third Principle - Honor All 119

Chapter 8: The Fourth Principle - Equality 137

Chapter 9: The Fifth Principle - Self-Control 151

Chapter 10: The Sixth Principle - Truth 169

Chapter 11: The Seventh Principle - Love 185

Chapter 12: Adopting the Divine Way 201

Epilogue: The Divine Way of the Universe 211

Glossary 215

Universal Truths 217

About the Author 221

Introduction

Looking *Within* will provide you with a new way to think and live so we can all raise the consciousness of the world and humanity. To begin, still your heart, get out of your mind, and listen within. You hear what you hear—nothing more, nothing less. Universal truth becomes clear the more you silence your heart and overcome your mind and body.

The truth is that you—your spiritual being—is 100% connected to God 100% of the time. You are one with the One. There is no separation except for the planes we live in—you in a human body and God in energy. We are one. There is no "you" or "I" or "they" or "them." We are we; we are one.

We are not disconnected. There is only "one" that encompasses all of us. You are not an individual human; you are just as you are—a human as part of humanity with humanity being the whole.

Think of it like this: A wave in the ocean isn't a separate part of the ocean, and neither is the ocean separate from the wave. The wave may be performing a different task at that moment, but it can't go off on its own. It is the ocean.

We are the same. There is no separate entity. There is one, one energy, one collective being.

You are one with the One. You are one with the Creator that is embedded into your DNA. But you are not God; you are a part of the whole.

You can never not be one with God. You are simply struggling with the various descriptions used for that oneness.

So please realize that, yes, you are a human, but you are also a spiritual being. In fact, you will soon realize as I did, that **you are a spiritual being having a human experience, not the other way around.** You likely understand that, but don't know yet how to express it. This book will help.

WHAT THIS BOOK IS ABOUT

Today, I am known as "the Renaissance Woman." I help others open their hearts so they can see the truth, open their ears so they can hear the Divine's whispers, and open their thinking so they can love again. But my journey to today and to writing this book began well over 25 years ago when I started my love relationship with the ancient lifestyle philosophy of Feng Shui. I embraced its principles, reordered my life, and filled it with harmony, love, peace, and calm. That early part of my journey led me to finding my quiet space within and journaling. It is through my quiet time with pen and paper that I discovered my deep spiritual connection and found messages within. Some of those messages are in this book and date back almost 20 years. Other messages on my journey led me to write other books or to study numerous ancient writings filled with wisdom and truth. Those numerous messages and studies have come together in this book.

Looking Within is about predicting the future, bridging the spiritual connection gap, and redefining spirituality. In essence, I'm unveiling the transformation of humanity … the transformation to consciousness … the transformation of the cycles, beginning and end, as within so without.

To begin, realize that God has always been connected to us, but over the years, humanity disconnected from our Creator. My objective is to help you build a bridge from where you are right now, reconnecting you to God, the One, the universe, and the cycles of the universe, the planet, nature, and humanity. **This bridge is desperately needed to enable humanity to become enlightened, and for those that are ready, help them to transform at the deepest level.**

A new Golden Age is coming, and this book will usher it in. The wisdom, knowledge, and truth the book brings forth will feed humanity for the next two ages. At the end of those ages, the information will need to be presented anew, so it is not forgotten and humanity doesn't need to fall so far down again.

This book is the gathering together of truth and wisdom of ancient and modern spiritual teachings and a holistic lifestyle, so that they become readily available for all of humanity to use in order to transcend their self-imposed limitations. The simplicity of these teachings will help transform our world from chaos and fear into hope, peace, and joy. It is focusing energy on the truth and on the wisdom of the East and West to serve others and help them find their path to enlightenment and transformation. What was ancient will become new, and will usher in a new era of peace and harmony.

The goal is to merge spirit (one spirit—everyone's spirit) with universal consciousness, with the One.

Silence is a key to the journey. Silence your mind so you can hear. Close your eyes so you can see. Open your heart to know the truth. It is here; you just need to let it in.

You'll discover that truth lies within and without.

My Philosophy

As I mentioned earlier, we are one. Your guides, your angels, passed over ones … we are all one with the One. The One is always within us, and we are and have always been one with the One. When we as humans reach enlightenment, we realize we are one with the One. The One is what you might call our Creator, the Divine, God, but our Creator is never disconnected from us. God is one with us. We are collectively one. There is always a direct connection. My purpose is to help people remember who they are, reconnect, and merge with the One and the universe.

Even though we often use the words "the Divine," "Creator." or "God," there is no Being per se; but there is a universe of energy created by a single energy source, which we are all a part of. There is an origination force called the One. We have never been separated from that

Introduction

original one source energy but as a society have often denied its existence or relegated it to the back room.

It's time that we truly understand both religion and spirituality. I propose that spirituality is the reconnection of humanity with our Creator and living a Divine lifestyle—of people wanting to learn and grow through spirituality, through an explanation, exploration, and personal experience.

In this book I will refer to religions as specific beliefs and life philosophies around the world. And I will be putting spirituality, not religion, into a new light of a "way of living your fullest potential."

This journey, this pathway, that you are about to embark upon has always been here. It has just taken this long to align the energy of the Earth, humanity, and the astrological clock to open the doors and usher in a new age—the age of connection—the connection of the past to the future and the connection of eastern and western spiritual philosophies. This is not only an alignment, but also astrological. All must occur in divine order.

The universe is moving into a new age, much like what the Mayan calendar predicted or the move into the Aquarius age on the zodiac. They both foretold the end of an old age and the beginning of the new age. Things will continue to get worse on planet Earth until the "good" on Earth can stand up and reclaim their control over the planet.

Our spiritual path, our destiny, is to bring heaven to Earth in this lifetime. Bringing heaven to Earth means "living in the moment in the sanctuary we've created, being productive, nurturing and loving others while remaining detached so we no longer use personal energy when nurturing and loving others."

Looking Within is filled with plain and simple messages and stories that will give you hope, peace, and a path forward. It will help ground you and move the collective back to gentler times or forward to better times. It is written in the stars that I will bring forth a new way of living (based on the Emerald Tablets and other ancient and contemporary spiritual philosophies)—a new lifestyle with appreciation for life, the spirit within. My number one objective is to help others build a bridge from where they are to connect with God and the universe. This process will make it safe to be a spiritual being in a human world.

Together we can help humanity learn how to play the new game for the greater good of humankind, the planet, and the universe.

Without HOPE there is only heaviness, negativity and despair. But HOPE is ETERNAL. It is a seed planted within YOU and is ALWAYS connected to the Creator. All of mankind IS connected to the UNIVERSE and EACH Other. Your Silver thread of HOPE will lead you to PEACE and JOY.

Part I
The Great Transformation

The world is broken. Our relationships are broken. Our sense of connection is broken. No longer do families truly connect. Instead, they are isolated individuals living under the same roof controlled by electronics and brain-washed by the establishment, with little or no respect for authority figures or each other. Friends no longer connect with each other, as they are so busy with work and life that they make time only for brief online contacts and occasional meet ups. The sense of connection in our communities is absent. Neighbors no longer respect or trust each other due to the fear instilled by media. Co-workers no longer share comradery and common ground. People are so divided by politics and race that they lack respect for self and each other. It is now a "you vs me" and a "them vs us" culture. The love, respect, and kindness we should all have for our fellow humans have been replaced by fear, anxiety, and chaos.

But this change didn't occur overnight. While this may seem like a recent phenomenon, it has a long history, perhaps hundreds or thousands of years. From Medieval Times back to the Roman Empire and before, the world was set up by power grabbing rulers who positioned themselves against everyone else. Society was based on conflict and competition, not commonality and connection. The rulers and the people with the most wealth, resources, and soldiers had the power. Everyone else was rendered powerless and condemned to servitude for eternity. Hence, victimhood was born.

Today, humanity watches helplessly as atrocities, hate crimes, and the demeaning of fellow humans occurs regularly, both privately and publicly in front of the camera. A demeaning, degrading, and controlling fear-based visual can flash around the world in a matter of seconds.

Commonality, looking out for each other, and having a central purpose for being have vanished like raindrops in the desert sand. This begs some key questions:

- What happened and why?
- Are we really helpless or can we as humanity stop this cycle and change for the better?
- Why are we, the collective we, here at this moment in time?
- Who are we?
- Who am I?
- Who are you?
- What can we do as an individual and collectively as a society to end the rampant fear, chaos, intimidation, and dehumanizing of humanity?

- Are you, am I, responsible for changing ourselves first, then humanity, to create a better world for our children, grandchildren, and great-grandchildren?
- Can we reclaim the world originally intended by our Creator—the world we lost sight of millennia ago?
- Is this the "way of life" humanity is supposed to or wants to live? One of decline, hatred, and survival?
- Or, is it our responsibility as citizens of Earth to rise up together and create a humanity built upon love, respect, commonality, truth, and wisdom? A world where all roads lead to the same place, reconnecting with our Creator and a better future for generations to come?

Before we jump into what our new lifestyle should look like and how to create massive improvement in the way humanity, nations, communities, and families treat each other, we need to choose to thrive, not just survive. We need to realize that the answers are not on the outside. We need to reconnect to our world within before we can improve the major issues facing the world without.

Part I is all about helping you look within to find your inner flame that burns brightly and awaits your arrival—that quiet and reassuring voice that will help and guide you along your path. Be prepared to find inspiration and encouragement that enables joy as you proceed on your personal intimate journey to reconnecting with your Creator.

Chapter 1
Tomorrow is Worth the Wait!

Reflect on the following questions:

How do you survive when the world is disintegrating?
How do you face tomorrow when you've lost everything?
How do you find light when you only see darkness?
How do you create a better tomorrow when everything you believe in is being destroyed?
How do you connect with others when they think a connection is electronic, not at the heart level?
How do you find truth in a sea of darkness?
How do you find any peace when everyone is thriving on chaos and disconnection?

The answer: Truth!

Truth speaks boldly, with conviction and an empowered, unrelenting compassion of the need for a spiritual reconnection—for spirituality. In order to survive, people need to put on a shield of truth, as truth leads to a spiritual connectedness to God and the universe.

So, what exactly is spirituality? It is an uninterrupted connection with the Divine life-giving energy force and the universe. Spirituality is the inward clearing process of removing old core beliefs that no longer serve us or provide us the openness to allow new energy and thoughts in. It is a cleansing of the old on the inside to allow transformation and to bring forth a new, healed, full-of-potential you.

UNIVERSAL TRUTH #1
YOU ARE A SPRITUAL BEING 100% CONNECTED TO GOD AND THE UNIVERSE 100% OF THE TIME.

Spirituality is "why we need to change" on the inside. It is about transformation, taking something ordinary or old and turning it into something better or extraordinary. Transformation used to be the silent secret of illumination. Today, transformation is change and improvement for the betterment of all. It is free from core beliefs, fear, and loathing. When we transform, we can get out of our own way, stop being our worst enemy, and allow our fullest potential to unfold.

The goal is to recognize there is a universal consciousness—an enlightened humanity. As more people transcend their humanity to a universal consciousness (as they go through this transformation process) we will move from the dark ages of humanity to a new Golden Age—an age where there is harmony between humanity, nature, and the universe. An age where there is more balance and less chaos ... more hope and less fear ... more commitment and less stress ... more gratitude and less anxiety ... more joy and less sorrow ... more love and less hate.

Too many people are stuck in "the mind," which creates separateness, problems, and conflicts. The being within creates wholeness; it is at one with the Creator, at peace. Enlightenment is the way to create harmony and joy. "Enlightenment (is) the end of suffering," said Buddha. "Enlightenment for all. Being is beyond the deep within, our deepest self, true nature." In the Bible, Ephesians 1:18, it states, "I pray that the eyes of your heart may be enlightened so that you will know what is the hope of his calling..."

Conscious living is sometimes defined as a group of like-minded individuals with similar goals, ethics, and way of seeing the world and supporting each other. Others see it as respecting and emulating what indigenous cultures and ancient wisdom figured out thousands of years ago—that we are all connected. Yet for others it means living consciously by accessing inner wisdom, insight, and intuition; allowing all of those to guide them; and being part of the consciousness of the energetic spiritual realms of the universe. Ultimately, when we follow our spiritual path, we find our consciousness.

Consciousness leads to enlightenment, harmony, balance, hope, peace, and joy; when enlightened, we are in harmony, at peace, and joyful. Everyone who is enlightened becomes a light worker by default, but does not have the same job or path upon awakening.

THE NEW ERA

In the new Era of Connection will come a whole new way of living, believing, thinking, and self-realization. Think of it like a Renaissance of Joy or a new Golden Age.

If you are questioning whether this is true, whether there really is a Renaissance ahead and if so how to move forward, then good for you. That's exactly what this book is meant to do—encourage you to question all the information we've been fed for millennia and bought into as truth. The real truth is out there; we just have to find it for ourselves.

Are you still holding onto a false hope that someone will save you? Well, here's some good news: Someone *will* save you. And that person is YOU. There are no white knights or saviors this time. The truth is that the only way we can be saved is to save ourselves.

That word "truth" can be loaded at times. There are organized portions of society that say, "Believe what you want as long as you agree with me." But you can't have it both ways. The only way to solve the problem is by everyone finding truth—not their truth, not partial truth, not your parent's truth, and not your professor's truth; rather, it's about finding **universal truth**.

This book will take you on a journey to find the universal truth. By studying the principles that lie ahead in this book, you will have a compass for living your life filled with peace, joy, and enlightenment. It will transform your thinking and actions while also transforming the planet into a healthier and better place for humanity to live.

But only you can do this, one by one, family by family, and community by community. The new Renaissance wave must become a tsunami—a wave so large it will crush partial truths, establishment's control, and prisons of mediocrity. As in Germany in the last century, the Berlin wall had to come down and merciless dictators had to be toppled. In this century we will see many more walls crumble as humanity rises up to take the reins of a newly found freedom based on ancient wisdom and truth from the universe. Dictators and fiefdoms will fall, causing temporary chaos. But freedom lovers and those connected spiritually will be prepared to step in and, like the Phoenix Bird, create a new society built on commonality, a spiritual connection, and respect for all, rather than deceit and control.

Millions feel the world is void of feeling and realize something is missing. It is as if we are longing for heaven to come down to Earth. The world is filled with chaos, fear, and hatred and is teaching future generations more of the same. Your voice is needed. Our voice is needed. People are waiting to hear the message of hope and peace. Many are actively seeking it but don't know where or how to find it. It's time to change all that. The wisdom and truth we all need is right here.

WHAT ABOUT GOD?

As we travel our journey together, I will talk about God—the Creator, the One Source, the All, Love, a Thought, the Original whole energy. Our Creator's thought formed the universe. Throughout this book I will be using many different names for our Creator as referred to in various cultures and ancient writings. God's house or abode is actually many houses (translated by ancient knowledge seekers as the houses of the zodiac). The current astrological move is from Pisces (fisher of men) to Aquarius (quenching the thirst of the world for a deeper meaning to life—a deeper spiritual connection).

Christianity and their version of God fed the world for 2000 years. Now it is time to move beyond religion and the use of intermediaries such as a priest or bishop to connect us with our Creator to spirituality. Today we can personally communicate at a moment's notice with our Creator. **We are moving beyond religion to a direct connection and knowingness!**

But people need to understand first that we are all connected. We are all our own savior, and we need to travel our own path back to the truth within. Step back and let go. Let human things melt away. Stand back and watch. Your first objective is self-realization, self-enlightenment. Then your objective will be to help the masses become enlightened and live by the principles of the Divine Way.

Collectively we are:

- Helping people to wake up to their spirituality
- Teaching individuals how to do good in the world
- Creating the new philosopher's stone to change the world for the better
- Creating a new Renaissance of Joy and moving the world into a new Golden Age
- Changing our physical environment to create calm and peace

- Changing the physical environment changes you
- Changing the internal self-environment creates perfect alignment, which yields balance
- Changing humanity for peace on Earth and changing the inner for spiritual eternal life
* Spending time in and loving nature to honor and care for nature
* Helping others become self-confident, self-realized, and transformed at the deepest levels
* Creating a spiritual inner-self personal transformation
* Creating groups of consciousness in humanity
* Teaching others how to overcome anything (drugs, dependency, depression, vulnerability) and create balance within
* Attracting like-minded people and groups
* Helping others merge their spiritual beings into universal consciousness

While travelling on your journey, be sure to smile, as it opens your heart to see. After all, every human wants to be:

* Unconditionally loved
* Living in harmony without strife on the outside
* At peace within and know they are safe

Focus on you, your path, your journey, and let life take care of itself. Each person has his or her own role to play. In order to do that you will have to be there fully first. At that point, you will be a spiritual being, a transformed being at the deepest level having a human experience.

In today's society, cultures are about religions and judgment of self and others. Many believe the mantra, "Our way is the only way." To them, anything else is wrong. We need to change this view, and that will only happen with the truth from the Source, the Divine, God, the universe. As you will see, different paths can lead to the Divine, to light, love, and to our inner self.

The revival of ancient wisdom and universal truth is all pointing to a massive spiritual awakening—within self, the family, the community, and then society. *Looking Within* is written to help society think in a new way. The goal is to help everyone find a better way to live their lives, get through the more difficult times, and make it easier to find joy, harmony, and happiness ... all the while understanding that it is *we* who control our lives, not others.

THE ULTIMATE CONNECTION

We are always connected to each other and our Creator. Yes, we (humanity) are all separated in our mind because of past teachings, but we are connected. We always have been and always will be connected on a spiritual and energy level. It is time to stand on our truth rather than have someone that is not in our life tell us what our truth should be. Their truth may not be in alignment with our truth.

UNIVERSAL TRUTH #2
HUMANITY IS ALWAYS CONNECTED TO EACH OTHER, GOD, AND THE UNIVERSE.

Focus on oneness. Everything, every blade of grass, every tree, every human is filled with the energy of oneness. Yet humanity lives as if everything is detached and separated—as if an action performed by one human does not affect anyone else, whether it is chopping down a tree or committing murder.

Unlike electronic things, which often have a few second time lapse before the power fully connects, you are always connected to your Creator, the Divine. Once connected, the millisecond you turn your attention towards something specific, the information is there before you even get there.

Being 100% spiritually connected all of the time is the precise objective. We need instant information and instant connection. We are always connected 100% of the time; most of us just don't know it yet. And we can never be disconnected from the Creator.

But we have been separated from the truth. Things distract, devalue, and lead to materialistic ends, wealth, drugs, always wanting more. Is that all there is? Open up to the potential of more spirituality through silence, not a life of materialism. What you see now is a seed being sown.

We all are:

- Looking for peace; rejecting chaos
- Seeking a peaceful way to live in the moment; anticipating the future rather than fearing it
- No longer believing the mind; we are seeking spiritually to find peace
- Abolishing victimhood; wanting accountability
- Getting rid of chaos; seeking balanced energy
- Eliminating intolerance; seeking harmony
- Rejecting survival; looking to thrive.

Do not question whether others are right or wrong; seek only the truth.

Your truth has changed many times through the millennia, but this time is different. You seek the Creator's truth, the truth of being and all things. You seek clarity and universal truth.

Why should people want to reconnect with the Divine, Love, Light, and the One?

- People believe in higher power; it's built into their DNA.
- People no longer want to be separated from God; they seek Love and Light.
- People are tired of mind games; they seek the truth.
- People don't want to be so busy protecting their life; they want to live their life.
- People want a life that is easier and calmer; they are fed up with lies and fear.

- Life is burdensome and chaotic; people want to be in control.
- People seek a better way of life; not a chaotic hate-filled way of life.
- People are never happy and don't have enough money; they seek fulfillment.
- People see their inner being deliberately hidden; they want to remember who they are and why they are here.
- People want a path to remembering what is important; it is written within.

This is very different than connecting to religion. In fact, religiosity is the box most younger generations are breaking out of, not into. Religion is the reason most wars are fought; people die and it is used to control others. Religion has lost its stronghold, and generations are fleeing but have nowhere to go. *Looking Within* provides them a landing space, a foundation to build their future upon to build the future of planet Earth upon.

Commonality reigns in all paths. The commonality in this book is that all paths lead to Love, Light, our Creator, the One, God, and it sheds light on those pathways. It is about coming into Oneness, the commonality of a new way of thinking, of forgiveness, of respect. Listen to the desert sands whisper, watch the ocean waves dance, and observe the birds soar in flight; simply feel the truth and wisdom come alive.

Like Christ said two thousand plus years ago, you need to be born anew, or "born again," to enter the kingdom of God. He didn't mean literally to walk into God's kingdom. He meant to gain wisdom and knowledge and an internal understanding of being always connected to the Creator, the Divine, the Great Spirit, God, and being conscious.

Forget about the how, who, when, and where—just be. Silence your mind so your heart can hear. Close your eyes, so spirit can provide you clarity.

There is a big difference between ancient teachings of truth and wisdom versus various religions. Also, there are definitely clusters of teachings that are from different cultural and geographical regions of the world. It's time to hear their wisdom.

Chapter 2
Why Change Must Happen

Most think planet Earth is a detached object, not connected to or responsible for anyone or anything. The truth is, Earth is a multi-complex, multi-dimensional organism in the universe of nothing but connections. Unfortunately, humanity on planet Earth is rapidly becoming disenchanted, detached, and disenfranchised with the planet and each other.

Some will have the same argument about humanity. Yes, there are individual humans but they are never separate from the whole or from each other. We all live our individual lives but do not realize how our individual lives impact others, our community, the world, and eventually all humanity. Our trap is the belief that we are singular and have the right to do anything we wish.

UNIVERSAL TRUTH #3
WE CAN DO WHAT WE WANT IF IT IS IN OUR BEST INTEREST, IN THE INTEREST OF THOSE SURROUNDING US, **AND BRINGS NO HARM TO OTHERS.**

This last part—bringing no harm to others—is of utmost importance. This is an ancient wisdom for our current reality.

We live in a world of ceaseless change and exponentially expanding technologies that further disconnect family, friends, business contacts, communities, and nations. Add to that diverse religions, cultures, globalization, virtual realities, and political power grabs and it's easy to see why and how society continues to drown in a maze of chaos.

Most people are very unnerved about all the chaos because they have not found their quiet space within. They are not connected to our Creator and the universe, and they feel very out-of-control.

Unfortunately, we have allowed this chaos to enter our lives and rule our thinking. But when we are 100% connected to God and the universe 100% of the time, we can totally find ourselves and take control of ourselves.

Finding ourselves first is the most significant task we have in front of us. If we don't know who we are, how can we possibly know what humanity, the world, and the universe are?

Why Change Must Happen

We, humanity and our individual selves, are in great need of taking control of our lives, our surroundings, and our environment.

UNIVERSAL TRUTH #4
HUMANS ARE DIVINE BEINGS HAVING A HUMAN EXPERIENCE, NOT HUMANS SEEKING A DIVINE EXPERIENCE.

First, we need to take care of ourselves by finding out who we really are—**a spiritual being experiencing a human life.** To do this, we need to quiet our mind, not allow outside influences to distract us, and then focus on that quiet voice inside filled with love, light, and truth. No, not the voice that says; "I can't," "I'm not good enough," "How dumb am I," "Nothing goes my way," etc. But rather that voice that speaks volumes about how to find hope, peace, prosperity, and joy—the voice that guides us, that makes us realize we are someone special on planet Earth and came here for a special purpose. No one is here just to be someone's son, daughter, spouse, teacher, or boss. We are all special with a spiritual job to accomplish as well as what we do daily as our human career. To make sure the voice you hear within isn't your mind acting as an imposter, refer to Universal Truth #1: You are a spiritual being 100% connected to God and the Universe 100% of the time.

We each are an important piece in the gigantic puzzle called humanity. What each of us does and becomes in our lifetime matters because there are no two people

Looking Within

alike. Each of us is as individual as our fingerprint. With that individuality comes a special function or job we are to perform while on planet Earth. This special responsibility somehow contributes to the greater good of humanity and the planet.

Take a moment to reflect. If Alexander Fleming hadn't discovered the first antibiotic, penicillin, millions would have died and many of us would never have been born. If Henry Ford had not invented the first assembly line for manufacturing, mass production would have not occurred, allowing for people to purchase products they need for reasonable pricing. If it weren't for Arthur C. Clarke, a RAF officer, and later John R. Pierce, AT&T's Bell Telephone Laboratories, sounding the alarm and pointing the way toward the need for satellite communications, we would be without cell phones, immediate video and televised production, and instant communications around the world. This data moves at the speeds of 186,400 m/s (300,000 km/s).

Each of these people not only followed their career path but also that inner guidance that took them to the next level of fulfilling a greater goal in life. They were the perfect people to fit into the humanity puzzle at those moments in time to create what was needed for the advancement of humanity.

BEWARE OF THE HALF-TRUTHS

The alarm bell that is ringing today is the vast chaos caused by political factions overtaking enormous pieces of the world's economy, health care, and the population itself because of fear and chaos created by drummed up pandemics, financial crises, and false political manipu-

Why Change Must Happen

lations. It is in their political and financial best interests to collapse the economy and control every aspect of humanity's lives. While they reap the rewards, we pay the price.

They are successfully doing this by using corrupt models of information and manipulated projections to create skewed results, then spreading this false information worldwide to sew further chaos and fear. This type of population control has been used for millennia by corrupt politicians, religions, and dictators.

This may seem like a new tactic in today's world, but in reality, this type of deception and control has gone on forever. Those in control or who want to be in control manipulate information in a way that makes them look like the preferred option. But if everyone were given the truth and acted upon it, then humanity would choose a very different course of action.

The battle here is about everyone having access to the truth, not half-truths, not bits and pieces of truth mixed in with half-truths and lies, but the whole truth. This is a form of transparency that should apply to all governments, all religions, and all political leaders. In the last century alone we've seen how these half-truths work to get people on the wrong side of history. For example, totalitarian leaders like Hitler cloaked hatred, aggression, cruelty, and racial contempt with the lofty ideals of faith, hope, love, and sacrifice for county. His effective half-truths and outright lies concealed the moral depravity, brutal racial cleansing, and vicious aggression of his idealism. Similar tactics were used by other leaders, such as Hidek Tojo or Mussolini during the same era. You can go back for centuries and see where fake-truth was used to sway populations. This took place sometimes through physical wars, other times through deception and wars of words.

Control by deception is hard for "we the people" to understand because internally most of us believe the truth is being given to us without any type of filter of deception or fraud.

Now is the time to wake up and realize we can no longer put our faith in the truth others speak, but rather go find it for ourselves. Truth is what this book is about.

There are seven basic principles of universal truth you can rely on (which we will discuss in Part 2). These principles are the process that will always lead you to the truth, both without and within, and will lead humanity out of OUR dark age.

A New Renaissance is Coming

The Black Death, otherwise known as the Bubonic Plague, in the mid-1300s was a pandemic in Italy, Europe, and Asia. It came to Italy via merchant boats from parts of Asia and Russia. Its devastation and unprecedented loss of human life not only transformed society, but also is credited for creating the Renaissance that lasted into the 1600s. I believe the 2020 Coronavirus pandemic that began in China and again devastated Italy (as well as the rest of the world) is about to bring forth a 21st century Renaissance of Joy and a transformative Era of Connection.

If physical contact of humans can cause such an explosive and traumatic transmission of a deadly disease, just think about the magnitude of good that can be created if we use that same connection process to find commonality and focus on the good in each other instead of the differences and perceived bad.

It is through direct connection with each other, finding the good in each other and the common ground, that we can create a better future and a peace-filled world. Connection is contagious and jumps like wild fires, engulfing families, neighborhoods, and communities in mere minutes. How much better would we as humanity be if we looked for that connection in each other not the differences?

Diversity has had its voice for quite some time but where has it gotten us? It has served to further separate us by not looking for the common good and teamwork. In families it has created an individual "all about me" experience, not the connection a family needs from young to old. Countries have a "look out only for themselves" perspective and are seeking to hurt others instead of looking for ways to find mutual benefit while caring for our planet.

The answer here isn't either/or. It lies in "what is best for all."

UNIVERSAL TRUTH #5
HUMANITY IS DIVERSITY UNIFIED AS THE HUMAN RACE.

Instead of leaders controlling their populations by keeping everyone at the lowest common denominator of health, income, and freedom, it is time for them to look out for the population by raising everyone to the highest common ground so they have the opportunity to thrive, not just survive.

Yes, the new Renaissance of Joy is coming. Over the next few hundred years there will be a transformational explosion of information in the vast and expansive fields of technology, health care, information, and science. Matching that explosion will be an equally massive change in societal interaction—the way we communicate, interact, and connect. Furthermore, humanity's connection and interaction will include an enormous spiritual component, one that will be based on truth and a direct connection with our Creator, the One, the Divine.

Gone will be the days of faceless humans walking down sidewalks with their eyes buried in a mindless piece of electronic equipment while their fingers dance on the screen and their messages ping back and forth. With the loss of eye contact and interpersonal relationships, mistrust will get a foot hold at all levels of society:

- Employee vs employer
- Parent vs child
- Teacher vs student
- Doctor vs patient
- Seniors vs youth
- Politician vs voter
- Bureaucrats vs the masses
- Government vs society

It's evident that we are well into this stage of mistrust. These relationships used to be untarnished and reverent. But the less transparent the connection, the less truth it is based on. The more electronic and impersonal the connection, the more people distrust and rebel against the established.

In many areas of life, we have more than surpassed that tipping point. And the more humanity is pushed to turn on each other, the faster the transformation and the new Renaissance of Joy will come. It will be unstoppable.

The Era of Connection, the new Renaissance of Joy, will be all about commonality, community, and spirituality, with spirituality being the common thread that brings everyone together and holds them together. This new society will strive toward helping each other and putting much greater emphasis on the cultural arts, ethical values, and a spiritual revolution that we haven't experienced since ancient times.

The reasons humanity needs to start their journey and a direct connection is to remember who they are. We will find that connection when:

- We are already on our spiritual path and seeking.
- We feel a longing or hunger for something more, but don't quite know what it is, or what we are missing.
- The Divine, God, the One has already spoken to our hearts and nudged us.

If seeking something but we don't know what, we will experience some of the following thoughts:

- "What is missing in my life?"
- "Do I feel like there is an empty hole in my heart?"
- "Is that all there is?"

- "Do relationships and social media make me feel empty, disconnected, unfulfilled, and alone?"

When we reach the point of seeking our direct connection to our Creator, we will experience the following. We will:

- Spend more time in reflection and meditation, which makes us healthier and less stressed.
- Discover we are never alone.
- Feel peace beyond understanding and a quiet sense of joy.
- Quiet our mind and receive answers.
- Always have someone to talk with.

Let go of what you think things should be, what they should look like, or how they should happen. Live in the moment so you can be free. Remove mental clutter so you can get clarity. Remove what no longer serves you so you can be well. Remove the old so the new can permeate your body and free your spiritual being.

Let go, let go, let go! Let go of:

- Who you were supposed to become; you are who you are.
- Time: time to get up, time to go to bed, time to eat, time to do.
- Old expectations, especially where family is concerned.
- "Would have," "should have," "could have" thinking.
- "If only" and "why not" thinking.

Transformative connection is about feeling, an inner knowingness. Feel everything! When we feel, we move forward. When we don't feel, we are stagnant; our body, our energy, and our spiritual being slows down. Close your eyes and feel the world alive around you. Tap into those feelings. It energizes and awakens all of us, bringing enlightenment. Reach out and feel in order to see. Feel, so we can breathe deeply what the universe has to offer. Feel, so we can truly connect.

Embrace Your Journey

We all have a direct connection within to our Creator, the Source of All, the Divine. My connection to God happens to be auditory. For you it might be a feeling, the written word, or a visual. It might even come in the form of dreams while sleeping. We are all somewhere on our journey. It doesn't matter how you get there, and it doesn't matter where you are on your journey to getting there. What matters is that you are striving, and that's being 100% connected 100% of the time.

Through our inner journey, we are to create a home for truth, wisdom, knowledge, and the ancient ways for humanity to come together. This will happen through our creativity, words, and artwork. We will bring to the masses a new understanding of what humanity is, how it should re-order its life to thrive in the new mindfulness world ahead, and how to make that transformation. We are not about being a psychic, an intuitive, a medium, or a channeler. We are about truth. We are about leading humanity forward into creating a better, more peace-filled world.

When we travel through the stages of spiritual growth, we often feel alone, unsupported, and lost, yet the collective, the we, are right here with you. The collective nurtures us, lifts us up, and surrounds all of us with love—the kind of love we experience as a spiritual community, the kind of love we enjoy when watching how they go from pain to love and light.

Be here; be now. Worry not about tomorrow or an hour from now. This is the moment. This is the one nanosecond of time we were meant to live.

Do not focus your attention any other place but here and now. It is truly the right place and time to be. All else does not matter.

We are living beings filled with the knowledge of creation and a commitment to perform our spiritual role on planet Earth. The knowing is flowing into our being. It is permeating our very essence. As we step into our new space and allow the universe to flow in and through us, we are one. We are one with our Creator, the Divine; our "One" is guiding us.

My spiritual destiny is to bring a set of principles (told through verse, prose, art, and stories) that people will easily understand—principles and a message that will give them hope where there is despair, peace where there is chaos, and joy where there is misery and fear.

Breathe; remember to breathe. It will serve you well. There is much negative energy around us and in the world right now, so breathe. Breathe in love and exhale chaos. Breathe in peace and exhale fear. Breathe in joy and exhale anxiety. This will help you remain focused.

Life has many distractions and gets in the way of our spiritual journey. We need to clear ourselves of pain to move forward. We need to tell our mind to step back. It is one of the team, not the leader. Our internal being is who and what we are, and that is where we come in.

Everything will unfold as it is supposed to. We are we; we are one. Clarity and focus are necessary for us to understand.

We are shifting; we are becoming us—the connected.

> The time for awakening is here.
> The Divine is by our side.
> There is no fear of failure.
> The words will flow, the knowing comes,
> and the being is.

Again, the goal for each human is to remember first that we are a spiritual being having a human experience on planet Earth. And, for the fulfillment of our experience we need to re-find our eternal connection to God and the universe. Through this we will find our destiny.

It's all about staying grounded and focused. Therefore, we need to:

1. Set our intentions on protection from all negative energy.
2. Clear our homes of clutter, negative energy, and things and thoughts that block the flow of new teachings, wisdom, and truth. For help in clearing your personal energy environment see *Feng Shui so Easy a Child Can Do It*.
3. Wear clothing, jewelry, and gemstones that keep us protected and provide us with uplifting energy.

As a society, we need to create a home that is our private sanctuary. Just as ancient temples and cathedrals were created as sacred spaces, ancient wisdom mandates our homes and bodies be our sacred space in the new Era of Connection. The eight components to creating sacred space are:

1. Taking time daily to go within and connect with the universe and Creator
2. Being at peace with all that is
3. Creating balance between creativity and logic in our brain
4. Living as if today is the only day that matters, because it is
5. Eliminating all negative thinking that holds us back or stands in our way
6. Being 100% connected within, to our inner voice
7. Creating surroundings that are uplifting, clutter free, and encouraging
8. Understanding that everything we think, say, feel, and do really does matter because that is how we create the future

We are about transforming lives and helping everyone move from the chaotic world we find ourselves in to a place of calm and quiet where we can hear the Divine's, God's, the One's voice and message.

Our soul is eternally connected for infinity. We are never disconnected. We cannot ever disconnect. We can ignore, not acknowledge, or be disconnected from our perspective, but we are always tethered to God's goodness, love, and eternal presence.

Our whole mission is to tie together into a pretty package the wisdom of the universe (not humanity and Earth) and present it in such a way that seekers will want to have what we have.

Our spiritual connection is:

- Being love
- Believing that we are heaven
- Knowing peace in our emotional self
- Living in every moment
- Embracing an abiding, non-judgmental love
- Being at peace at all times
- Knowing our life is cradled in the arms of our Creator
- Loving all we touch
- Doing no harm to others
- Having a song in your heart
- Feeling that no harm can come to us
- Living our truth within

It will all start to make human sense to you soon. The puzzle pieces from ancient texts, such as the Emerald Tablets, the Bible, Buddhist traditions, the Bhagavad Gita, astrology, Native American beliefs, indigenous tribes, meditation, Feng Shui and other esoteric information, will come together and form a complete picture for everyone that seeks.

Now that you know why change must happen, let's uncover how to do it.

Chapter 3
The Roadmap to the Future

As a part of humanity, you need to be who you are; there is no other human like you. Be the best you can be. There are no mistakes. You were born who you are, someone special to serve a unique role in the humanity puzzle of life. You chose you, so you need to love you as you are in this moment in time. If who you are is the person you wanted to become when you were born, then you've accomplished your first objective in your life. That's great.

Are you the person you agreed to become spiritually? Have you taken any time to seek your divine self—that spiritual being that is within wanting to help you every step of the way to find your way back home to your Creator, the universe, the Source of All?

It is when your physical and spiritual beings become aligned that you find your true self, peace, and joy, no matter what the circumstances.

Seek and you will find your spiritual being hidden within all the noise, chaos, and earthly distractions. Most people advise you to look in all the wrong places to find spiritual fulfillment, places such as groups, social media, electronic devices, cultural and political organizations. But few tell you to look within. It is within, in silence, where you find truth, wisdom, empowerment, peace, love, and joy. No one is powerless or insignificant or an accident. We are the bridge to the future.

Put your throughs aside and silence your mind so you can hear. Close your eyes so you can see. Focus on your heart so you can connect with your Creator, the First Source, God, the One, and the universe. You will find the answers, the truth, your path back to your spiritual being. You are much more than you've been led to believe for millennia.

The time has come to step into the future, to create the world we really want.

Release Your Fears

Isn't it time to get rid of fear—fear of others, fear of the powerful, fear of the government, fear of your neighbors, fear of your friends, fear of your enemies? Fear is what separates us. The more fear the powerful feed into our minds, the easier it is for those in control to succeed and manipulate us to do their bidding.

We need to turn off their faceless electronic censorship megaphones and look within. We must listen to our voice within to learn the wisdom and knowledge we need as a society to overcome the lies and half-truths so we can thrive. It is all written within. The secret is to silence the deafening noise on the outside and the inside so you can hear the calm steady voice within. This is the voice that encourages and inspires you to improve self and others, and bring no harm to anyone.

Some will say, "What do you mean, the voice within? That's nonsense," or "That's all that metaphysical stuff. There is no such thing." The truth—whether you learn it from western teachings such as common law, Christianity, Judaism, indigenous tribes and Native American wisdom, or eastern teachings from various eastern culture philosophies like Buddhism, Taoism, or Hinduism—comes from a voice within or messages from on-high. It is time to find the commonality of humanity and do what serves all humanity, the Divine, and the universe the best.

Once we connect with our inner voices, it is much easier to quench any fears, to find our way forward, to find our eternal connection to the One, the Divine, God, our Creator.

This is where the roadmap to the future begins. This is the first step on our path as we strive to discover and create a better future. This is the path that leads us to the truth about how important it is to keep our freedoms, justice for all, respect for self and others, and honor for all beings and things. This is where our spiritual compass resides. This is where we learn what constitutes universal truth and wisdom, what is being controlled by others, and just how little we control ourselves.

Humanity can no longer rely on others to look out for our best interests while they focus on obtaining more control and wealth for themselves. Catastrophic events like a World War, a major planned or unplanned financial collapse, or a pandemic set the stage perfectly for either complete control and a mandated acquiescence of society or an uprising of the masses reaching for higher ground, for something better they wish to leave behind for their children, grandchildren, and beyond.

Now is the time! A great Renaissance lies ahead for the making. Each of us in our own way will play a role in forming a new society built on a foundation of ancient wisdom and truth, and then together we will apply it to our modern reality. But to begin, you have to find silence to release your fear. Once you've taken your first step on your path, your journey unfolds when you:

- Connect with God and the universe 100% of the time and humanity as needed
- Communicate with God, the universe, and others 100% of the time
- Change the planet and humanity, one tree, one bird, one person, one community at a time, through your words, creations, and actions.

SPIRITUALITY SETS YOU FREE

As I've noted several times and will continue to emphasize, everything is connected. Nothing stands alone. All is one, and one is all. One way to refer to this process or lifestyle is living in harmony with each other and nature. Turning chaos to order in the universe through connection yields peace-filled continuity, and peace-filled continuity enhances your ability to find a deep, meaningful connection with your Creator and the universe.

Who are you taking orders from about the way you live your life? Are the messages coming from inside or outside? Are they coming from your Creator, your quiet voice within, or society? Or are they coming from your parents, your siblings, your buddies, or the media? If they are not coming from our Creator and the universe, then there's a high chance you're feeling lost and have no plan to find hope, peace, and joy.

The seven spiritual principles we will expound upon are found in almost all ancient philosophies, which become the foundation for all things that follow. They are known as universal truth and wisdom. *Looking Within* is about building a bridge to the future based on the wisdom of these seven principles in the chapters ahead. It also speaks about what separates you and the judgment by self or others. This way of connecting is the way to joy. Joy isn't just a day, a moment, or a thing like a collection of memories or watching your children grow up. This book has a message of hope, peace, and joy to give to millions who are seeking or just waking up and realizing something is very wrong with humanity today.

For our purposes moving forward, spirituality is:

- The increasing awareness of a higher consciousness
- 100% connection to the Divine and the universe 100% of the time
- A deep abiding peace within
- Unconditional love
- Seeking wisdom that serves the greater good of all
- Doing no harm to others.

In today's modern society, millions of people have stopped going to their places of worship and following spiritual values because they don't enjoy getting up early on a weekend morning, feeling like they need to get dressed up or dressed period, going through the hassle of getting their family together to get them to a worship service, and not really enjoying the experience. For them, they feel there is no reward for the effort.

They feel no obligation or commitment to our Creator, the Divine, and see no benefit to a worship service or living by the lifestyle recommendations of their particular religious or spiritual choices. In reality, the lifestyle recommendations have nothing to do with whatever place they worship or don't worship, but rather are guidelines for the way a society should live their lives.

For example, Christianity has been teaching the Ten Commandments for thousands of years. They are just as relevant now as they were in the beginning. But I don't necessarily consider those Commandments only belonging to a religion. I believe they are more about how humanity should treat each other and live within a society. They are about societal order or an ethical code for living. It is important to separate what is religion (without) and what is spirituality (within).

Others go to religious services during particular times of the year, such as during Christmas, Hanukah, Ramadan, or Easter. They feel there is a real specialness to going to a spiritual building or place and being surrounded by other like-minded people who enjoy the service or the music. In contrast, others who have attended services for years don't go any longer because of the new contemporary music. It resonates very differently with them than what they were used to hearing when they were younger. They feel that it doesn't take them to that place inside where they feel connected to God.

The truth is, music is a creative energy and helps you access your soul. Music is an important component to your connection with your Creator, whether in a place of worship or in your home sanctuary. Music can paint a magnificent picture of harmony and connection through its lyrical and sound resonance. If you quiet your mind, you will hear the Divine speak through the melodious sounds.

Prayer is an equally important component. It allows you to be quiet, to go into yourself and your mind, so you can have a direct conversation with God. Yes, the minister or religious leader is saying a prayer, but you're not necessarily listening to what he or she is saying. You can have your own prayer time. Be encouraged, go within, and move into a more meditative or deeper prayer state.

The more you move within, the more you learn. The fact is that all the information in the universe is ready for you to access. You simply need to reach out with thought and capture it into your memory bank. It will not clutter your memory space by downloading. The need and desire for truth is growing exponentially. Many people are searching, but don't know what they are searching for. Civility, truth, belief in something greater than they are—all are missing in the world today and will get worse until the message of hope, truth, and peace become the commonality bond for humanity.

The only threat to our future is our indifference to the past, which has been distorted and erased where possible. This only serves to distract and divide us and is why connection is so important now. The Era of Connection is about living a spiritual life while on Earth so you can transition into a permanent spiritual world in the afterlife, and be part of the majestic magnificent world of eternal peace and joy.

How do you know when you hear an answer to your prayer or some other type of communication? Sometimes you get a strange feeling, and you think to yourself, "That doesn't feel right." So, you steer away from whatever that is. Or you may get a feeling of peace and calm and think, "Oh, that feels really good," and you take positive action. That is a message from within. Other times you may receive a message through a dream, a picture, a visual image in your mind, or a song that pops into your head. People are different; they receive messages in many different forms.

Also, you don't need a cathedral or a cold and ostentatious building to communicate with your Creator. All you need is a place that is quiet, peaceful, and serene so you can get inside yourself, calm your mind, and just have your own time with God, the One, our Creator.

While a physical place of worship isn't necessary, there are good reasons for worshipping in a cathedral or designated places of worship. The windows, the arches, and the spires of medieval places of worship were symbolic of sacred geometry that connected the people that entered those churches to their higher selves, to God, to worship. For example, the 12 loops that went around the big cathedral windows represented the 12 apostles, or the 12 symbols or houses of the zodiac. Spiritual symbolism was often done through sacred geometry and through numbers to connect with God. The spires reach upward toward heaven and were used to help people become more connected to God. So it wasn't just about the buildings or the stained-glass windows; it was about the connection to the Divine, The One, our Creator.

Today, it is still about the connection, but this time it's not about bringing the connection through a cathedral or temple, but bringing the connection into you, your body, and through you to reach others. Your body is your temple and you make the connection within. Heaven on Earth is programmed into every human's DNA. Once humanity catches up, heaven will be on Earth collectively.

THE CONNECTION PROCESS

Be the someone you were meant to be when you arrived on planet Earth. Be you! The importance of self plays a key role here. Be an individual of value because there is no other person exactly like you. You matter, we matter, humanity matters. None of us were ever a mistake. We all have a spiritual role to play on planet Earth. We each are an integral piece of the humanity puzzle. We each need to play our role well because the future of humanity depends on each person doing their part to leave this world a better place than before we came.

Know yourself. Each person needs to learn who they are, what their beliefs are, what their strengths are, and that the connection to God is real and eternal. The whole idea here is getting people away from society and its beliefs, and turning us all back into spiritual individuals deeply connected to the Divine and the universe.

Accessing your higher self or inner self is where you begin. Some people are already at this stage because they took their first steps days, weeks, or years ago. Other people will need to be spoon fed and given step-by-step instructions. It doesn't matter where and when you began your journey or how far along on your journey you are. What matters is that it is important enough to you that you are beginning and working with the tools of quieting your mind, listening for that quiet calm voice within, and connecting with your Creator.

How do you have an intimate relationship with God? How do you become who you're really meant to be 100% of the time? People need to ask questions like:

- Do I do things a certain way because it is the way someone else told me to do it? Or is it the way I want it done?
- Do I think about things a certain way because this is what I really think? Or am I letting other people's opinions and influences overpower my own voice, my internal voice?
- Do I do things because Aunt Susie, Grandma, a teacher, or a media commentator told me this was what I should do?
- Are my spiritual beliefs based on who I am?
- Do my spiritual beliefs really ring true with me? Or do I struggle with them?

Ultimately, this questioning leads you to who you are. It helps you realize whether your beliefs are coming from God, or if they're coming from others, authoritarians, politicians, or a person behind the pulpit.

Creativity, such as through painting, sculpting, writing, dancing, or playing an instrument, is another way to connect with the universe. Flexing your creativity opens the communication link between you and the universe or God, and the information just flows. Creativity also helps quiet the mind. And it is through quieting the mind that you can attain oneness. The quieter and more creative you become, the more you control your mind, and the more you evolve spiritually.

Once you've found your connection, be 100% connected. Let that inner voice be louder. Really hear it. Really pay attention to it. Know that it's real. It could also be a feeling—one that is so noticeable that you change the action you were about to take. Feelings like that should never be ignored. You can choose to act upon it or not, but don't ignore it, because it is a direct message to you. Pay attention to your nightly dreams. Keep a journal by your bed so you can write down key images or themes or words you remember from your dreams. All these feelings and dreams are your inner voice that tells you, "Don't say that; don't do that; don't go there; or today is the day you need to go to see your ill grandmother." To receive messages like this, you don't need to get plugged in. You already have a 24/7 direct WIFI connection with your Creator. You have a personal hotline.

Your spiritual journey begins when you are 100% connected to God and the universe 100% of the time. We are not only connected to the Divine, but also to the universe. Our Creator made the universe, and into the universe built universal laws, truth, and wisdom that cannot be broken. If it were to break, the universe could not exist. These laws, truth, and wisdom apply equally to all humanity.

We need society to become more about "I am," not in a selfish or conceited way, but in a way of "I matter," or "I am important." As in, "My life, my time on planet Earth, is important and I am an important piece of the humanity puzzle. The small things that I do matter. They may seem small to me, but to the universe it's my contribution. I am not insignificant. I matter."

However, as a society, we've become more modern, more sophisticated, and more educated. We've drifted and have even been pushed away from the spiritual side of us. This has been going on for such a long time that we no longer even know how to access that part of ourselves. If we did, society would not be engulfed by fear and chaos, and we would all be happier. There would be less disease. There would be less mental illness from stress and anxiety. We would have a better understanding of how to fulfill our destiny, if you want to call it that, and tap into our talents and our strengths. We would also have a much higher and better understanding of who we are as human beings, and how we contribute to the universe.

It doesn't matter what era or millennia we are discussing. These basic universal laws and principles are relevant no matter what the timeframe. This spiritual relationship and the direct line of communication is with our Creator, the One, the Great Spirit, our guiding force in the universe. The glue that holds the universe together are the ancient laws of truth and wisdom.

Many ancient spiritual cultures had more of a direct line of connection to God than our current society. For example, Native Americans never heard of Christianity until the white people came and talked to them about God and Jesus. They had their own form of spirituality, their own connection with the universe, their own connection with the Earth. They had very strong beliefs regarding what you take from the Earth and that you give back to the Earth. Their original way of life was far more spiritual and connected to their Great Spirit than Christianity's God. They spent time honoring nature and quiet time with the stars.

It is during those quiet times you get an idea that springs into your head, and you realize, "Oh, I never thought about it that way." This is another way God communicates with you. Or maybe it could even be a couple of days later, when somebody says something to you, and you think, "Oh, okay, I get it now." That's another message from the Divine.

Look Within
Look within to find all answers
Look within to see what you seek
Look within to align the human with the spiritual
Look within to create your wealth
Look within to become who you are.

When humanity discovers its direct connection with the Creator, the One, it's like the relationship of a parent and a child, or twins, or siblings who have a deep connection. They almost know what each other is thinking. If twins are very connected, and one asks the other a question, they both seem to know what the answer is going to be before the question is even asked. It is this type of spiritual, heart connection we seek. You don't often learn how to have that kind of a spiritual relationship, or that kind of an eternal connection with the Divine, the One, our Creator in most churches or religions. Religions tend to separate God and the people. Instead, spiritual relationships are a direct line of communication with the Divine, the guiding force of the universe.

EMBRACE SILENCE

When trying to create such an intimate relationship with our Creator, people often ask, "Is silence a prerequisite for finding your inner self, your voice within, your direct connection to the Divine, the One, the First Source, God?" Yes. Silence is the foundation most people use when initially trying to find their inner connection. It is very difficult to hear the voice within when there is chaos and noise pollution invading every area of your life.

UNIVERSAL TRUTH #6
SILENCE IS THE FOUNDATION FOR
SPIRITUAL CONNECTION.

The trick is to learn what works for you. Right now, you may be thinking that silence is silence, but some people can find silence in a crowded terminal and hear their voice within. Others need absolute quiet with no distractions or with soft music playing in the background with a candle burning in order to get connected; other options may include walking in nature or sitting on the beach or lakeside. The question isn't so much where but rather *what* works for you. Think meditation or prayer. What do you need to do to get into that type of silent space and then stay there for a period of time?

The Roadmap to the Future

When you find your silent space, it's time to get busy. Quiet your mind and focus only on the silence and your breathing, with eyes half open or totally closed. If you prefer having a candle burning then focus on the center of the flame. In the beginning, your mind will wander; gently send the random thoughts away and focus on your breath. Continue to focus on breathing. You can also focus on the tip of your nose to gain access to your inner self. This process simply takes practice. You will get there. You can set a time length if you wish or you will just know when you are done. Be sure to keep a notebook and pen nearby so you can write down anything you want to remember following each session. This is how you start your roadmap to a better future.

Since I don't practice meditation as much as others, one of the ways I find my inner voice is by creative journaling. Creative journaling is not the same as a journal of daily activities or a diary of sorts. This type of journaling requires quieting your mind and listening for the message being given to your heart from your guides, angels, your Creator. You know it's the truth when it is in your best interest and brings no harm to others. I journal daily before my day gets too hectic. Sometimes life gets in the way and I don't get to my journaling as often as I'd like. It is those days when I feel less centered and in need of reflection. I feel a bit lost until I resume my fully connected communication link.

For me, journaling is a two-way street of 24/7 communication connection. I ask questions, and I get answers, or I get what is standing in the way of the answer. Then I have to deal with that before I can move forward to the resolution of the original question I asked. There have been times in the beginning where I've had to take care of a number of "somethings" standing in my way before I got the answer to the question I originally asked; but the answer always comes when I am ready to receive it.

One of the biggest questions you need to answer now is, "Are you ready?"

Chapter 4
All Divine Paths Lead Home

Now that you've learned the importance of quieting your mind so you can seek your inner voice, it's time to begin at the beginning. After all, how can we accomplish anything in our lives if we don't begin and don't have clear objectives? Many people ask, "Where is the beginning—the starting point?"

Your starting point is right where you are at this moment. That statement holds true for all of humanity, whether a child, a senior, someone controlling others, or someone being controlled. We all begin exactly in the moment and place when we discover it is our turn to take that first step on our journey to find the light within, the truth, and our eternal connection.

The most important step you will ever take in your life is this first step. So quiet your mind, go within, and find your eternal connection with the Divine. Once taken, this first step will change your life forever. You will view humanity and the planet through a different lens, and in many cases, see truth for the very first time. What you see could be dramatic, shocking, and eye-opening, or it may not surprise you at all. Since truth is written into our DNA, on some level you will recognize it and not be surprised.

TRUTH TEST: *All paths lead to your spiritual home as long as they are based on universal truth; ideas and actions, when conceptualized and put into words, should apply equally to all and harm no one.* If the messages you are receiving do not pass the truth test, do not trust them. Re-center yourself on your inner wisdom until you find universal truth.

Others who have totally bought into the chaos, prejudices, and lies of those in control will be shocked in disbelief and dismayed that their feelings and opinions might not be in accordance with the truth. They will be in denial. This will cause them fear and anxiety until they gain perspective and an understanding of the truth within. This book is not about telling someone he or she must change, but rather it is encouraging all to go within and find the truth—not their truth, but the truth and wisdom of the universe.

The important thing here is to begin. Don't be afraid of today. It is the best day of your life when you finally realize there is more to living than just surviving the day or going through the motions while feeling unloved, disconnected, and unappreciated. In the process of finding your way to truth, you release stress, anxiety, and guilt, replacing them with peace, love, and joy.

There is no greater first step than to find truth within, as this guides us to our personal eternal connection to the One, First Source, God, the Divine. Once we've begun that journey, universal truths, wisdom, and the Divine Way will be revealed. We will make decisions that not only lead to a better life for us personally, but also help create a world that is for the greater good of humanity, our planet. and the universe.

When we take that first step it is truly about us stepping on our path to enlightenment, connection, and oneness. But in reality, each of us that takes that first step is joining millions of others who are also committed to creating respect, honor, peace, and justice for humanity. This is not a noble goal but rather an awakening of humanity and a return of planet Earth to its original grandeur when equality, balance, and love were the norm, not the exception.

Seeing the Commonality

For thousands of years people have believed that we could not communicate directly with our Creator, God, the One. We were told we needed someone better than us to be an intermediary, a link to make that connection. Although there was a belief in monotheism, in ancient times it was the temple priests who controlled everything; in medieval times it was the bishops; today there still is some sort of leader who stands between us and the Divine. This Judeo-Christian western system is based in part on a "one Creator, grace, and return to heaven philosophy."

In other parts of the world, people were taught that there is no creator deity, non-theism, but rather life is beginning-less. There is an empty void in the universe and the cycle of birth and death never end with karma being the controlling factor. Its basis is spiritual development, self-responsibility, and attaining deep insight into nature and life. They do believe in "morality, meditation, and wisdom leading to enlightenment." Other Eastern belief systems share similar values of self-accountability.

Many of the indigenous tribes, aboriginals, and Native Americans believe in distant land formations, in the sky, the Earth, and nature, all deserving honor and respect. They believe in a sacred Great Spirit and the inanimate as well, such as mountains, rivers, lakes, and clouds. Their beliefs included "qualities of goodness, wisdom, and perfection."

While studying various philosophies of living and ancient wisdom, I realized that they all did share several beliefs or principles of wisdom and universal truth. These principles bring together the best of eastern and western philosophies, providing a road map for thriving in the next millennia and beyond.

It is through the commonality of these principles that a new way of life filled with peace and joy is attainable. It can be formed and molded back into planet Earth's original design—a way of living our lives to our greatest potential filled with hope, peace, and joy.

Today, we are a society greatly in need of ancient wisdom and universal truth. *Looking Within* helps us build a bridge for humanity to seek a new, upgraded, and vastly improved world based upon universal truths and inner wisdom, not cultural and religious differences or political authoritarianism.

The seven universal principles in Part 2 are based on commonality and truth, not differences. None of the principles prevent you from following your existing religious doctrine unless it stands in the way of or covers up universal truth. In that case you will need to seek inner wisdom and guidance to find the path you need to follow.

The Divine Way begins with the understanding that we are eternally connected 100% of the time with the One, God, First Source, our Creator, and the universe. Since not all philosophies have this as their basic premise, this is a huge first step for some. For others it will feel natural. In my case, I can never recall a day when I didn't know my Creator, the Divine, God. My Divine Being has always been in my life. I may not have understood what that meant for a number of years, but I was never without knowing my Creator's presence.

Start with YOUR Connection

All humans are connected to God and the universe in some way, whether consciously or unconsciously. The question is: how connected? Is it a one-way connection? Are you connected at 3%, 29%, or have you reached that sweet spot of 100%? The connection is eternal. It is always available to you. You don't need to be in a certain location like a hotspot; you don't need earbuds or an overhead satellite. You just are, always have been, and always will be connected.

With this hard-wired connection nothing is impossible. In fact, all is possible as long as it improves humanity and brings no harm to others.

To make this first step—the return back to the Divine—easier for all, there are different pathways to find the Divine, Love, Light, the One. And while they may be different, they all lead to the same place. Besides an inner knowingness which happened to be my experience, there are three commonly used methods for seeking and finding your connection.

1. Creating balance by eliminating chaos in your life leads you to your internal connection within.
2. Surrounding yourself with silence by eliminating all noise pollution leads you to truth.
3. Remembering who you are, a child of the universe and the Creator, leads you to ultimate love.

The method you choose doesn't matter. We all need to find the method that works best for each of us. The important thing is to begin. While this may be your official starting point, you actually began when you read the first few words of this book.

Right now, quiet your mind and reflect in silence. That is the only way back to the truth—the truth you were born with, the truth in your DNA that you know to be true.

You have the strength of the universe built in. You are strong. But we are stronger together. We are one. We are you and us, all connected for eternity. We are the collective humanity. We have the power to create, manifest, and to bring about change to our families, community, nation, and humanity.

Open Your Heart and Create Your Change

The heart is where you are eternally connected, not in the mind. The heart is where you connect with other spirits on their personal journeys. It is where you find what you call a "soul mate." It is where that gut feeling comes from. It is also where your internal fight or flight mechanism comes from. The heart is where life begins, and where it ends. When it beats is when life begins—when it stops it ends. All ancient wisdom is in the heart, your heart, my heart. The DNA of the universe is in the heart. The important point is to find your key to accessing the heart, which brings you to today. Keep your mind closed and your heart open so you can hear.

Choose freedom from being tied down to the mundane. Let your heart and soul soar. Remember the words of Johnathon Livingston Seagull: "Don't believe what your eyes are telling you. All they show is limitation. Look with your understanding. Find out what you already know and you will see the way to fly."

Remember, everything you need and seek is within.

Move. Get going. Your journey is unfolding faster than you are moving. Take time for your heart to think, time to wander and reflect, to visualize and see with great clarity. You will change your life when you eliminate the chaos and create a new language in your ever busy mind based on the concept that **what you think, say, feel, and do today creates your future**. Your future belongs in your hands.

UNIVERSAL TRUTH #7
CHANGE IS THE ONLY GUARANTEED CONSTANT IN OUR LIVES.

TRUTH carries wisdom and power. It is a cycle that is difficult to break and powerful when used for the good of humanity. It is about transformation. Truth, wisdom, and power when used for the betterment of humanity are unstoppable.

It's about transforming lives and helping humanity move from the chaotic world they find themselves in to a place of calm and quiet where they can hear their voice and God's voice. It's hidden in all messages, yet found in none. It is universal truth, but seen by few and understood by even fewer. The discovery or answer lies in ancient tablets and books. It is truth. It is the message everyone seeks. This one single thought is the glue that opens this book; it is its philosophy. It flows throughout the book and closes the book with the challenge to begin now. Tomorrow has arrived.

What we are creating with our deep meaningful connection is Heaven on Earth. Look into the eyes of a newborn child; you will see Heaven on Earth. Their eyes reflect having just arrived from heaven and seeing you.

- Heaven on Earth is an abiding non-judgmental love.
- Heaven on Earth is life cradled in the arms of your Creator.
- Heaven on Earth is knowing peace in your emotional self.
- Heaven on Earth is doing no harm to others.
- Heaven on Earth is feeling no harm can come to you.
- Heaven on Earth is living your truth within.
- Heaven on Earth is a song in your heart.

- Heaven on Earth is loving all you touch.
- Heaven on Earth is being in love.
- Heaven on Earth is being at peace at all times.
- Heaven on Earth is living in every moment.
- Heaven on Earth is you, and you are heaven.

The connecting link between the physical person and the spiritual one is the heart; the heart partakes of both the material and immaterial qualities. The desire for higher knowledge must develop within and strengthen the will to be able to concentrate all powers of being on and in the plane desired, in this case bringing the lifestyle qualities of heaven to Earth.

Bringing heaven to Earth is an important lifestyle change. Creating a calm peace-filled physical environment based on the Feng Shui principles of using positive energy to create desired results is not enough to really enjoy a full, stress-free, prosperous life in the new millennium. It takes more to offset the self-imposed, over-scheduled lifestyle filled with cement cities, and a fast-paced chaotic world. The fears are many. It takes so much more to compensate for this self-imposed, stressful, anxious world people have imprisoned themselves in.

Chaos is chaos. It can be clutter in your home or office, it can be negative thinking, or it can be overuse of social media. It can come from the people you hang out with, the negativity on the television and in movies, or built into video games and the ever-present smart phone and social media. Ultimately, it doesn't matter what the root source is causing the chaos in your life, but rather how you react and respond to it. Everyone has a coping system based on their personality and astrological sign they were born under.

Chaos is often created by world governments that can be horrific, undulating turmoil of evil and tyranny trying to permeate every corner of the Earth, every home, every family, and every mind. Chaos is having a black cloud of doom floating overhead that is churning and about to boil over. Its turbulence and great upheaval will continue to cause much fear and grieving, which continually feeds the fire of the monster. It consumes hope and joy by converting them into anxiety and fear.

Wisdom conquers all with universal truth as our foundation, our eternal connection as our guide, and love as our beacon of life.

You Can Take Control

You need to be full of positive energy, as chaos is on overload. You need an abundance of energy to create calm, and to help others get in control of their chaos, lack of control, and connection with others. Meaningful connections with others are a devastating absence in so many lives and is a direct result of the chaos that has permeated every aspect of society. For example:

- Seniors living in assisted living facilities or their own homes where no one ever calls or visits
- Children being in day care programs or after school programs instead of being raised at home
- Babies being cared for during the day by strangers
- Children being taught in schools filled with fear, bullying, and chaos

- Adult children expecting parents to come to their rescue
- People of all ages constantly isolated and in contact on social media, but never connected
- Millions with no hugs, eye contact, or touch decay from within
- Without connection, touchy-feely connection, there is no balance

Many feel forced into the above scenarios due to how society is set up. And while it pains them to have to take certain measures, they do it because they feel they have little choice or control. This is why you need to align your inner self and personal surroundings with your spiritual destiny. The antidote is to find ways that provide hope for the future. **Where there is hope, there is no fear. Where there is light, darkness cannot exist.**

DO IT NOW! Now is what is important because that is where you are called to wake up and to work. Now is where life is—not tomorrow, not yesterday, but NOW.

Take Control

Take control of your life
so it becomes what you choose.
Take control of your life
put aside the unimportant.
Take control of your life
put aside the unnecessary.
Take control of your life

put aside others.
Take control of your life
put aside Earth thinking.
Take control of your life
put aside the human ego.

The power of thought (WORDS) matters. It creates everything, including Heaven on Earth.

Do the important first, and you will thrive. Do the urgent first, and you will only survive.

God is the creator, the one source, love, thought, the original whole, energy. *Looking Within* is about quenching the thirst of the world for a deeper meaning to life, a deeper spiritual connection. We are moving from the Age of Pisces, fishers of men, to Aquarius, the transformation of humanity back to spirituality. What worked in the Piscean Age no longer works in the Aquarian age.

The messages from ancient texts and tablets will speak to your soul. It is your time to learn so you can step into the light and receive great understanding and wisdom. Humanity's and your spiritual agreement is to "be 100% connected to God and the universe 100% of the time and teach others how they can find their own connection."

The great search for light, life, and love begins on the material plane carried to its ultimate end—connection. Its final goal is complete oneness with the universal consciousness. The foundation in the physical is the first step; then comes the higher goal of spiritual attainment.

Yes, you can be and are 100% connected to your Creator as well as all of us, much more so than you realize. It is an eternal connection. You don't need to be in a certain location, gender, race or class. You just are connected, always have been, and always will be.

Calm and focus are your mantra for days that seem out of control. Maturing in the spirit brings great wisdom while enabling you to deal with fewer choices. Our job is to create a bridge to encourage enlightenment, to create a pathway for humanity to come into alignment with Earth, others, the environment, and the universe. When you have no plan, you accomplish little.

Make a Plan

When you have no plan, you lose your focus
When you have no plan, you get distracted
When you have no plan, you get discouraged
When you have no plan, you get lost.

A Human Destiny

Remember:

- No two people are in the same place on their journey.
- Everyone has freedom of choice no matter what they are taught or encouraged to do or be.

- Different responses to life circumstances result in vastly different outcomes.
- Harmony can be found in diversity if one chooses.
- Joy in such diversity is the reward from balanced harmony should one choose.

All seven principles of the Divine Way do just that; they build alignment with self, others, the environment, and the universe. The end result is a new harmony—a way of life that overcomes self-imposed limitations, cultures, and prejudices.

Today, society is one of status, diversity, and isolation. We live in an immediate society that has no patience and needs immediate gratification. It's a society greatly in need of ancient wisdom for the current reality.

Put earthly things aside so your truth, wisdom, and knowledge can appear front and center. Spiritual oneness is a goal of the world, but it is also necessary for oneness in the family, community, humanity, the planet, and the universe.

All paths lead to the same place, a 100% connection to the Divine, our Creator, God. Those paths are not to be confused with religious paths. Those spiritual connection paths are:

- Creating balance by eliminating chaos
- Surrounding yourself with silence
- Remembering who you are

None of the religions collectively teach all three, but any of the three will lead you to your eternal connection to love, light, the universe, God, and the Divine. It is the spiritual principles this book lays out, not just the kindness to humanity, that are sorely missing in the world today.

Stay focused, get in alignment with who you are, and start your journey on your path to enlightenment and 100% connection to your Creator 100% of the time. The best of everything happens, comes into focus, or becomes reality when alignment and enlightenment is the focus of your world.

Discovering your INNER voice, your HIGHER SELF and your SPIRITUAL connection is very EMPOWERING and joyful. The RICH colors of birthing energy SURROUND you. Finding the DIVINE, you are filled with the EXCITEMENT and ANTICIPATION of a HOPE-filled future.

Part II
The Seven Principles of Universal Truth

Once you have stepped on your path, started your journey, moved past the darkness, and discovered your deep eternal connection, it is time to learn how to maintain your connection and move forward.

There are seven principles that form these teachings based on ancient wisdom and universal truth. These principles create a bridge for humanity to a new life, an enriched life, a new norm—to live a Divine Way and transform the world into a better place to live, work, raise a family, and re-connect with the universe, the One, God, the Divine on a personal level.

The Divine Way provides humanity a way of living so individuals can reach their greatest potential. It's a way to overcome fear, replacing it with peace and respect for all creation, including others, nature, animals, and the Earth itself.

Change is coming! There is a new normal ahead. You can be prepared to welcome its bold arrival or hide in a corner and fear it. It is up to you to determine whether it will be a stressful time for you filled with anxiety, or more like a reunion with a long-lost friend providing you a calm assurance that all is well if you go with the flow.

Since you can't stop its arrival and you can't change what it is, the next best option is for you to change and meet it head on. Happily greet it so you and society can move forward to find calm, peace, and joy.

Think of it as a puzzle. Each step you take, each principle you adopt and make part of your lifestyle, will provide you the wisdom, knowledge, and sustenance to move forward to the next puzzle piece or principle on your journey.

Those in control, be they governments, bureaucrats, leaders, cultures, or religions, need to understand the world has moved into a new age. Some may refer to it as an astrological change to the Age of Aquarius, but I prefer to think of it as the time of bringing planet Earth back to its original glory and moving humanity forward to its destiny where peace, wisdom, and truth reign.

Are you ready to move forward, to find the life you came here to live? It is time for us to unchain ourselves from our self-imposed limitations and take responsibility for our future. It is time to remove the things that cause chaos in our lives like fear, anxiety, and cultural conditioning, and replace them with hope, peace, and joy.

Chapter 5
The First Principle: Wisdom

Time doesn't change its rhythmic movement, but all things change in time. All societies have an ebb and flow with a yearning to create balance.

Humanity cannot survive without inner peace. What is blocking your pathway? Is it cultural traditions? Family beliefs? The ideas and opinions of another individual you've taken into your confidence? Political beliefs? Or maybe yourself? Inner peace comes from accessing Truth from our quiet space within and applying WISDOM.

UNIVERSAL TRUTH #8
WISDOM IS KNOWING THE TRUTH AND APPLYING IT TO ALL YOU THINK, SAY, FEEL, AND DO.

Our society tends to focus on the differences in humanity, not the overall commonality. These differences include things like culture, race, religion, age, gender, victimology, and politics. Now is the time for this emphasis on differences to change! The emphasis needs to be placed on the commonality of humanity, not the differences, in order to enable life to move forward and thrive on planet Earth, not just survive.

But before you jump off the deep end, be sure the pool has enough water and is deep enough for that dive. Nothing is as exhilarating as taking that first plunge, but if you're not a swimmer or a pool person, fear and anxiety will take control. What then? Do you even consider the dive? What about using a safety device like a life vest? Would you make that dive now?

Maybe you like skydiving, hang gliding, skateboarding, or mountain climbing. All of these are filled with adventure, risk, and an overwhelming amount of fear. But when you overcome that fear and accomplish the task, you feel exhilaration and joy. This is exactly the same sense of exhilaration we all feel when we've accomplished the impossible or overcame our fears and anxiety to finally find the prize on the other side—namely peace, joy, and enlightenment.

But getting to that place takes wisdom. It takes wisdom to make life and death decisions. It also takes wisdom to lead a fulfilling life where you are in control of you.

The journey to ultimate peace, joy, and enlightenment is fraught with just as many road blocks, hazards, and anxieties as diving into a pool at the deep end, skydiving, or mountain climbing. And just like those accomplishments, achieving this one goal of an eternal spiritual connection to God, the One, the Creator, the Divine, for eternity is exhilarating beyond expression.

EMBRACE YOUR UNIQUE JOURNEY

Where you go on your journey, how far you travel, or how long it takes you does not matter. Only your success and arrival at your eternal connection, enlightenment, really matters. It is what you were born for—to find your way back home to discovering that you are a spiritual being and always have been, not just a human. It's about realizing that you are 100% connected 100% of the time to your Creator, where you have complete understanding and knowingness that surpasses human understanding.

Making this life altering change and discovering this newly found gift of enlightenment permeates the very fiber of your existence. You become a re-energized, renewed, and regenerated human prepared to fulfill the spiritual role you committed to upon entering humanity on planet Earth. Now you are fully equipped to discover the importance of who you are as a spiritual being on earth. You are about to become the someone you were meant to be.

Everyone has a duty, a function, or a spiritual role to perform while on Earth that contributes positively to the whole of humanity and the universe. No job is too large or too small; all are equally important. For example, my spiritual role is to create a bridge for humanity to reconnect to our Creator and the universe, which will help others discover their path and journey. Your spiritual role is something unique to you. Without you there might not be a major scientific breakthrough that saves millions of lives. That would be a major loss in the humanity puzzle. Perhaps you could be the firefighter who saves the life of a child who grows up to be the first human on Mars. Whatever it is, your specific spiritual role in life will be absent if you do not understand that you are an important person in the human race and have something special to contribute.

Some may argue that they didn't ask to be born and don't owe anyone anything. That is not the point. Everyone who came to planet Earth is here for a reason. Everyone (even YOU) has a spiritual role to perform and needs to find their way back home to the One, the Creator, the First Source.

Enlightenment is knowing who you are—a spiritual being having a human experience—and why you are here. Humanity has had a taste of enlightenment in the past from Ancient Egyptians to Native Americans. Each of these lifestyles knew that their roots came from the universe and the most important thing they could accomplish in their lifetime was to find their way back home, to their spiritual home in the universe that is.

This thought process has become so foreign in the last few millennia. Only now are we starting to understand the enormous power of the universe and the First Source, the Divine, the One who created it with a thought, a word, an action.

Take time and reflect on the magnitude of creating the whole, ever-evolving universe from a thought and that we are a part of this creation. Talk about change! Not only are we a part of this magnificent creation, the universe, but we as spiritual beings also have a role to play as part of humanity in moving everything forward to a more prosperous peaceful era in a timely manner.

THE PATH TO WISDOM

The time has come on planet Earth to heal and build a bridge to the future. Enlightenment is one of those steps or principles on the road to a new, peace-filled tomorrow. Think of enlightenment as 100% connection to our Creator and 100% harmony in all things and all energies. Some examples are:

- Universe balance – the Divine and humanity
- Gender balance – masculine principles (self-reliance, logic, intellect, and action) and feminine principles (love, nurturing, intuition, reflections)
- Human balance – yin and yang

After studying many cultures, indigenous tribes, native Americans, aboriginals, ancient Egyptians, eastern philosophies, and western religions, I saw that WISDOM was a foundational principle to all.

Wisdom is often described as the quality of having not only knowledge, but also the good judgment for using that knowledge appropriately. **For the purpose of this book, I am going to further qualify WISDOM as having knowledge and judgment AND using it to improve self and others without harm to anyone.** Here's an acronym that shows the importance of wisdom:

W	Wisdom is universal truth
I	Information consistent through eternity
S	Source of it is the universe
D	Defines all action
O	Other source is within
M	Make time to learn and absorb before taking action

Seeking wisdom is an important first step on our spiritual journey. Wisdom can arrive in many forms. When we seek wisdom we must look inward, not to the outside world and others. Yes, we can glean wisdom from others, especially older generations filled with years of personal experiences, prayer, meditation, and culturally handed-down messages through the millennia of generations. But choose wisely. There can also be a lot of misinformation built into that wisdom. That is why we need to place great importance upon our own personal journey—the journey within that leads us to all of the universal principles, enlightenment, and the ultimate place of peace filled with love and light.

Realize, too, that just because some things have been practiced in our culture, society, or religion for thousands of years doesn't mean they were built upon the principle of WISDOM. Some practices were used to control populations, create fear or chaos, and make people think they are victims. They wanted the masses to depend on those "in control" in order to keep humanity disconnected and divided from each other. Their goal was to force a combination of fear and chaos. That is not wisdom.

In order to find true wisdom, we need to quiet the noise in our lives and our mind. It's essential that we quiet the noise from everywhere and everything, including those who are not looking out for our or humanity's best interests. Be sure to include electronic devices and social media where there is no guarantee of truth.

Often, it is the small things in life that distract you from the important. We find this occurring at home as well as at work. For example, in the workplace, you may be working on a major project with a completion deadline of 24 hours. Even with a closed door, associates knock and automatically enter, insisting their question or problem is more urgent than what you are doing. Or, your phone constantly rings or chirps with text notifications interrupting your focus and concentration. The same happens at home. Perhaps you are running a specific errand to help your child finish a project for school when the phone rings. You answer it and are greeted by your friend who claims to urgently need your help doing a laundry list of errands, expecting you to make yourself available. You become so involved with her needs that you overlook the original reason for your errand until you get home.

Whether at work or at home, you need to define your priorities and not let other things get in the way, especially electronic technology. When the urgent(s) become the important(s), you accomplish less and have less energy. **Always do the important things first, not the urgent!** Here are some suggestions to help you shift your focus:

- Create wellness in your life; it is natural to be well.

- Envision your regenerated life filled with wisdom and enlightenment happening, detach from all else.
- Stop over-thinking and second guessing, it leads to the wrong direction; it leads to a hamster-like wheel of life.
- Dump the mental negative loop of thoughts that constantly bombard you; eliminate negative thinking.
- Live in the NOW; your life video is of the past, not the present, and the future is not guaranteed.
- Meditate, watch a candle flicker, move to a space of quiet peace; give up the reins; find a place of ease, not dis-ease.
- Strive to be who you are, not perfection.
- Live your own story, not someone else's; be the someone you were meant to be.
- Align without and within for true balance and harmony; there is no toxicity.
- Remove negative thoughts; focus on peace and calm, which is joy.
- Honor your Source, Creator, God and be grateful; show gratitude at all times, this creates a fruitful gratitude attitude
- Acknowledge that there are parts of you that you like and love; those are the parts you want to keep. Eliminate the parts you want to get rid of.

Learn from Ancient Wisdom

Humans long for less chaos in their world. They want less stress and upheaval, and yearn for peace and calm. Ancient societies were designed to live in harmony with

The First Principle: Wisdom

each other and nature. The goal was to care for and protect each other—to nurture when needed, guide when necessary, but above all, love one another as they love themselves.

Many cultures such as Native Americans, the Mayan, and the indigenous natives of Australia, the Amazon, Africa, and elsewhere believe that humans are directly connected to all things in nature, the environment, and the universe above. They show great respect for the four cardinal directions, North, East, South, and West.

Many ancient-based cultures place great emphasis on the wisdom of Feng Shui, which is an ancient lifestyle philosophy using positive energy to create desired results. Through its principles, you can take control of your life, reduce stress, and create a peaceful refuge, a sanctuary at home and a more productive workplace. The result of following its principles will be a more calm, prosperous and peace-filled you.

These ancient cultures also have reverent respect for not only the four cardinal directions, but also the four intermediate directions, Northeast, Southeast, Southwest, and Northwest. They used the directions to honor planet Earth and nature, as well as a teaching tool. It was all about relationships—how to create balance in the individual's life, with other individuals, within their community, and in their spiritual relationship. All of this leads to harmony and balance within the family, the community, other nations, and the universe. They look upward to the sky to find reverence, a spiritual connection to the One. They honored the earth and its directions as part of their ancient wisdom to create peace and harmony on Earth and within the universe.

Looking Within

East	communication, the rising of the sun, birth, growth, the new
South	warmth, home, passion, good fortune, luck
West	commitments to the earth to provide sustenance, creativity, and family
North	foundation for humanity, career and spiritual life, enriching lives

Just as knowing directions is important for a traditional physical journey, like a road trip, knowing the directions and their spiritual connections is important for guiding our spiritual journey.

There is nothing that separates us, except your physical body is on Earth. On a spiritual level we are together and in one spatial realm or frequency. *Looking Within* is about teaching peace through balance, harmony, and spirituality, not just physically and intellectually, but spiritually as well.

Know that you are always divinely connected. You are never alone. You are eternally connected. It is built into your hard drive and permanently hot-wired by the Creator of the Universe, the Source of hope.

Another ancient piece of wisdom heard often, but not recognized as such, is "As above, so below." There are many ways to define this universal law, but for the purpose of this book we will define it as "what happens in the heavens above (meaning the stars and planets commonly referred to as the study of astrology), happens below (on Earth)."

A good mantra would be: "I am 100% connected to God and the universe 100% of the time. That is when I perform best." That is the first thing you need to fully recognize as truth. When you know you are 100% connected to God, the One, the Divine and the universe 100% of the time, you are on the path of "I am."

"I am" is:

1. Being 100% connected to God and the universe 100% of the time
2. An effortless flow of peace-filled, vibrational energy
3. Knowing that you are a spiritual being having a human experience
4. No fear of failure
5. Fulfilling your spiritual destiny during your human experience (not to be confused with what you think your human commitment is to God)
6. Unconditional love
7. Being part of God, and God being part of you
8. Knowing you are in the presence of your creator at all times
9. Living every day as if it is your last day as a human
10. Seeking truth and finding it in all you undertake

The Process

Your future is now, in the light in front of you, not in the past and not in the darkness.

You attract what you focus on. You create all of your tomorrows by what you think about today. That is a universal law, one that if followed will help you create what you desire, as long as it is in harmony with the universe. It will help you attain a life filled with joy and peace. If you focus on all that you don't have, that is exactly what you create, more of what you don't have. Therefore, stay in the present and observe what your mind is telling you. Change what you focus on and you will change the results.

There is great joy and pleasure in knowing you are plugged into the greatest power—the power of the universe, your Creator, the heavens above.

"Train me to be in conscious awareness in present time" is another good mantra to help keep your focus on the present. Conscious preventative awareness causes you to:

- Link consciously with Divinity for empowerment
- Take charge consciously of your situation or proposed situation
- Take charge of being the director
- Be conscious of your thoughts and actions
- Create a new future by using change wisely

Joy is an attribute you will need to experience more. Through joy you can see the future. Through joy you can experience the present. Through joy you will find peace within and all that you seek.

In fact, joy is the answer to every question.

- Does it bring you joy and brings harm to no one? Then do it!
- Does it get you closer to your goals and objectives, which bring you joy? Then do it!
- Does it increase your connection to God and the universe? Then do it!

The First Principle: Wisdom

This is the magic formula for life. If it brings you joy directly or indirectly doing no harm to others, then the answer is yes. The only other consideration is timing. Is now the right time to do this, or will it hinder you from completing something more important or take energy away from something you are trying to complete?

Treasure each day and find joy in each day so you can progress. Move into your new space so life can unfold.

Time does exist and has always existed. Without time, there can be no order, no law, no beginning. It is the separation by time that the universe exists. First, came a thought of creation. For that to be, the first time had to have a follow up action of what came next. It takes millions of years (time) for planets to form, to change, to sustain life, to remain in their exact orbital positions.

That is why commitment, discernment, and wisdom are so critical for creating the future, your future, the future of humanity.

What Difference Would It Make?

What difference would it make in the world if you didn't exist?
Your destiny would go unfilled.
What difference would it make in the world if you didn't take your first breath?
The lives you have touched would not find peace.
What difference would it make in the world if you wouldn't have discovered your path? No one would receive the information you are to deliver.

Looking Within

What difference would it make in the world if you wouldn't have taken your first steps on your journey? You could not show others the way.

What difference would it make to the world if you didn't find your inner heart and soul? The world would be without your hope of a better future to come.

In a world of cement cities, noise pollution, electronic interference, and isolated environments, it is difficult to find peace. When you are connected to God and the universe, you are connected to everyone, everything, and all that is for eternity. This is truth, whether you as a human acknowledge it, understand its existence, or know nothing about it. Everyone is always connected to everyone, everything, and the All, all of the time.

This book's message will bring peace to those who listen and will share it with humanity. Not only are you unique and a beautiful one-of-a-kind gem, but you are also perfect in your own way. Help complete others in the map of humanity. We all have our own shape, vibration, and destiny to fulfill on planet Earth. Become enlightened so your unique puzzle piece can live in the hearts of everyone.

With true wisdom, the mind disappears and you become one with the all-powerful energy of the universe, the Divine, the Great Spirit, First Source, the One.

The First Principle: Wisdom

Wisdom leads to Enlightenment.

Chapter 6
The Second Principle: Respect

Light is the goal you seek to attain. It is your eternal connection—the eternal flame in your heart.

Those with wisdom understand that we are all born on planet Earth as human individuals no matter the race, culture, ethnicity, or religion. And every individual requires respect because they are a new human created by the Divine, the One, the First Source, God, the Great Spirit, or Original Thought.

UNIVERSAL TRUTH #9
ALL HUMAN LIFE IS PRECIOUS AND A GIFT FROM GOD.

Looking Within

Everything that is—everything that exists—was created first by a thought and then by the action of our Creator. According to most ancient teachings, all things began in that original thought. Even science is inching its way in this direction versus the Big Bang Theory, according to mathematicians, molecular biologists, intelligent design scientists, and science/religious writers. They have invoked the probability arguments in criticisms of biological evolution.

Many years ago, when I was writing, the following came to me with great clarity:
"If God, the Divine, the Source, is eternal, infinite, omnipresent, truth, love and loves me, LOVES ME, then I must deal with the fact that first and foremost, I must love myself. Therefore, everything I think, say, feel, and do matters…because that's how I create my future. And, if I love myself, a human, I am compelled to love others; humans also created by the Divine."

This thought process builds the bridge to connection and hope and peace for humanity. This message of loving self and others became the basis for a twenty-year search for the answer to: how do we as a society build a bridge for humanity to get from old beliefs, selfishness, and prejudice to treating others as you wish to be treated. That search led me to the principle RESPECT.

UNIVERSAL TRUTH #10
TREAT OTHERS AS YOU WISH TO BE TREATED.

The Second Principle: Respect

When we live our lives using the ancient philosophy of "do unto others as you would have them do unto you," and apply the concept that every life is a creation of the Divine, there is no room for discrimination, judgment, or control by others. The truth is that humans are 100% equal in the eyes of the Creator, the One, or the Great Spirit. When we acknowledge and embrace this truth, it eliminates all separateness and mandates unity.

In some ways, it is the human version of "cause and effect." For example, if you love yourself and your body, you will care for it. The effect is a healthier body filled with calm and peace. Likewise, if you abuse your body, it will decay and become diseased. The larger effect of caring for yourself is when all people and societies act in loving and calm ways toward others. As each person embraces this truth, love, calm, and peace expand. On the flip side, if people act in controlling and hateful ways toward each other, then chaos, hate and fear expand.

This simple principle, RESPECT, provides the bridge for humanity to become a universal family. When expanded by humanity to its fullest potential, this change will create a new world that will force dictators and leaders filled with poison to flee and governments that don't respect human life to crumble. Darkness cannot live in a humanity filled with light. We see this happening everywhere on planet Earth. Toxic leaders and governments that do not put their people (human individuals) first, or those who turn their people against each other for purposes of control, will and are falling from power. Respecting each and every human individual from the first heart beat to the last must be a priority for families, communities, countries, and the world if we want to survive in the short-term and then thrive in the long-term. This change must begin now with each of us. If we do not respect and protect each other, who will?

RESPECT THE BALANCE

Nothing happens by coincidence; nothing happens by chance; nothing happens by accident. Even an accident isn't by accident. Everything that happens is a result of the choices you have made, thoughts you have had, words you have said, and actions you have taken. Some results may take mere minutes to manifest, and others years. That is why commitment, discernment, respect, and wisdom are so critical for creating your future and the future of humanity. Life is always a balancing act between focusing on fulfilling your commitments versus being flexible enough to discern what distraction is important enough to temporarily put your commitments on hold and give your attention to. By applying and incorporating this respect principle to your life, you will reduce chaos, distractions, and stress while dramatically increasing calmness, prosperity, and balance.

There is great order in the universe. All that exists is only because of universal principles or laws, as they maintain order and harmony. The universe cannot exist in chaos, nor can a human. The more you allow outside thinking to influence you inside, the more chaos grows and controls your life.

It's all about the flow—the unending connection to our Creator and the universe. The flow through that connection goes from the universe to you, and then from you to the universe. What happens to one happens to the other; as above, so below; as without so within; cause and

The Second Principle: Respect

effect. The spiritual connection is eternal even though the human experience is not eternal.

Much like in the universe, time is involved. A human is born (time), grows up (time), and then becomes an adult (time). We have historically celebrated human time with birthdays (time markers). The significance about a human's lifetime is that the only time that matters is right now, today. Yesterday is gone; it is the past. Tomorrow isn't here yet. If you focus on the future too much, it brings about fear of the future, or at minimum, a waste of today. That's why today is the only time that matters. It is the present. It is where all humans should live. That's where you live the best life possible.

It takes either a very spiritual deep understanding of this truth, or the simplest understanding of a child, to love and respect who you are and the impact that has on others and the universe. When rulers and leaders continue to feed hatred and fear, love is blocked out of our lives. Love can overcome anything, but not for those who have never seen it in action, never experienced it, or have been told it doesn't exist. Love does not exist for those who have had the seeds of hatred sown within by others from the moment of birth. Love is foreign for those under oppressive rule, or those with parents who do not implant and reinforce right versus wrong, good versus evil, hope versus fear, and love versus hatred.

So many have lost their way; others don't know there is a way; and some are desperate to find something, anything they can hold onto. People are in great need. The greater the turmoil, the greater the need. The answer is found within. Connect with the One, the Creator, the Divine and you will find the love and light to sustain you so you can thrive—so we can thrive. Once you find love and light, respect comes naturally.

Respect Yourself

As I was contemplating the way forward in 2007, I made the following decision. I chose to have my personal energy field to be my sovereign space. No one was allowed to step into my space without my permission, and if I did allow them in, they must leave behind no footprints, no residue, and no connections. No trespassing! My space—my energy—is solely my own, and no one has permission to enter without an invitation. My field is a sovereign orb of energy. I can enter other's fields if they allow, and join in union and communion, but when I step apart, I am totally free and totally clear. This truly became the official beginning of both my journey and this book.

As I've said before, the number one objective of *Looking Within* is to help others build a bridge from where they are to connect with God and the universe and follow their path based upon that connection. Respect of self is vital for making this connection.

Focusing right here, right now, provides you immense self-respect. Control your thoughts. Do not let your mind wander; that does not serve you well. What you think creates your future, so focus your thoughts only on what you want to create. Thoughts are what create results. Think wisely and carefully so you can create what you want, not what you don't want. Respect yourself enough to focus on what is best for you.

The Second Principle: Respect

UNIVERSAL TRUTH #11
TO BE A CONSCIOUS CREATOR YOU NEED TO ALWAYS BE IN CONTROL OF YOUR OWN THOUGHTS.

Manifestation happens when you place your focus/energy on what you desire; where you place your energy becomes your reality. If you want to create your heaven on Earth, that's where you need your focus to flow. That is how you respect yourself first. It is very difficult to respect others if you do not respect yourself first. You can use a mantra such as "I choose to surround myself with my 100% connection to God and the universe. Together we will thrive."

Here are some examples of focusing your thoughts so they embody respect:

- If you want to create beautiful art, focus on creating beautiful desirable art.
- If you want to write a bestselling book, focus on creating your book.
- If you want to be spiritually connected 100% of the time, never leave the connection space while you move to the other thoughts and projects.
- Focus on this minute, not any other.
- Focus on today, not tomorrow.
- Focus on what is at hand, not what was, or might never be.

Quiet your mind and you will find it. Control your thinking, and you will get there. Close off your left brain by touching your right brain, and you will succeed. Breathe; breathe in the new and release the old.

UNIVERSAL TRUTH #12
WHAT YOU FOCUS ON BECOMES YOUR REALITY. YOUR EXISTING REALITY IS WHAT YOU'VE FOCUSED ON IN THE PAST.

Focus your energy on things that matter, like wisdom, respect, love, and light. Place energy on only your objectives. Remove energy from things that you fear. Reduce energy on things that don't really matter. Life is quite simple: Give energy to the important things and withdraw energy from the unimportant. Focus your mind on these three thoughts to truly respect yourself and humanity:

1. Recognize your spirituality—that you are a spiritual being having a human experience and that there is something more to life.
2. Transform your thinking from being a human body to becoming a spiritual being eternally connected to God and the universe.
3. Through the transformation of self (including thoughts), realize, understand, and become I am.

Through the many universal principles and laws laid out in tablets and ancient manuscripts, you can find a

The Second Principle: Respect

personal roadmap that will not only help you along the way on your spiritual journey, but also will give you peace and joy within, plus balance and harmony without. The journey is somewhat different for each of us, but we all wind up in the same place and live life based on the same universal truths and principles. Respect will help get you where you want to be.

R	Reflect on the flame in your heart; it reveals the true you.
E	Eliminate chaos and stress; it is easier to find respect.
S	Spiritual growth and respect begin in the heart; silence is golden.
P	Place your hand over your heart; you show respect to the truth within.
E	Engage all your senses as you seek; respect flows from all.
C	Choose to silence your mind; the flame within is where respect begins.
T	Take time to reflect; respect the special person you are.

Searching for your voice within and finding your connection with the Divine is the ultimate form of self-respect. It takes unconditional self-respect to reach the next level of your spiritual growth. Meditation is a vehicle to connect to the voice within. Meditation, with the purpose of gaining wisdom and knowledge from the universe that you can apply to the human experience, helps you cultivate a mindset of respect for all. This is when you're on the path to do the following:

- Being 100% connected to God and the universe 100% of the time
- Teaching others how to find their own connection
- Creating heaven on Earth for self and others
- Providing hope to others for the future
- Creating an abundance for you and for your family

At birth, every human being is filled with God's love, but most never experience it long enough to make it a permanent part of their life. In my case, I always knew, even as a young child, that I was connected to God and I never let go of that belief. Years passed and it would be dormant as life consumed my daily activities, but I knew I was connected. I didn't hear the voice within then, but I just knew. I always knew to respect that internal knowingness of the Divine even when I didn't understand it. You, we, are all filled with the love of God. God's infinite love is eternal, always has been, and always will be.

The other thing meditation teaches you is to play an active role in listening. If you don't listen in the moment of silence, you will miss the journey.

Part of the respect process is to use Active Spiritual Listening to:

1. Make a conscious decision to be 100% connected 100% of the time so you can be an active listener to spiritual guidance at all times.
2. Have an intense personal relationship with your thoughts, mind, and ego. They should not be in control of yourself; your spiritual self must be in

The Second Principle: Respect

control in order to proceed on your journey or down your path.
3. Be 100% aware of every time you and all of your thoughts move away from your spiritual being. Gently bring yourself back and re-focus on your active listening.

Breathe

Breathe; your body needs to regenerate to give you peace
Breathe; without it there is no human life
Breathe; look deep within, the answers are all there
Breathe; it is the key to your future
Breathe; it is all written;
you need not worry about the past or the future,
Breathe; focus on your destiny, others await your arrival
Breathe; you have little time to learn everything you need
Breathe; your future awaits you; you need to be prepared
and full of truth, wisdom, and knowledge to serve others.
Breathe; take it all in
Breathe; breathe in the health of life
Breathe; others and the universe
await your entrance.

HONE YOUR FOCUS

As I said earlier, focus on the important, not the urgent. Respecting self comes from the wisdom of knowing what is important and requires your uninterrupted attention. Create a list of the most important tasks for each day and rank them in order of importance. Rewrite your list so the top five things are the most important for you. For example, if meditation is on your list, then it should be one of the first five things you do. Take time and schedule for the urgent, but do not allow the urgent to control you. The urgent is never so important that it should take place of the important, unless it is a true emergency. The urgent always happens. In fact, it comes in waves. The important is what must take priority. The calmer your surroundings and your personal environment, the easier it will be to remain focused on the important.

Energy is always flowing to the list of important things to do. There is always energy flowing upward from planet Earth to the Divine, the One, and then downward from the universe, the Divine, the One, God. Your energy is always connected with the Divine and the universe whether you realize it or not. Respect is acknowledging the importance of this connection.

When you respect who you really are, a spiritual being having a human experience, you transform yourself from the physical self-level. That's when you are connected and can transcend your humanness. Ancient wisdom and universal truth are about transformation and enlightenment, not the alchemical type of transformation, but rather returning to your spiritual being in the human body versus a human being with religious or spiritual aspirations. If you are a bit confused at this point, below are a few definitions that might provide you clarity.

- Spirituality: The increasing awareness of a higher consciousness.
- Astrology: The roadmap in the stars of your destiny.
- Metaphysical: The interaction of all that is.

Ancient wisdom and universal truth give you a roadmap on how to proceed on your journey to accomplish your complete transformation and return to your spiritual foundation. This is respecting who you really are.

Mind and ego must take a back seat to all you think, say, feel, and do. Mind and ego serve only selfishness, conceit, and arrogance. They have no regard for your spiritual self and others. They have no right to control your spiritual self, your flame, your light within. They need to be subservient, to serve and support your spiritual self and all you are.

How do you think like a spiritual being when your human mind and ego always want to be in control? The answer again is simple.

- Being empowered yields confidence and inspiration
- Creating a sanctuary yields value
- Feeling worthy yields an anxiety-free life
- Being nurtured yields hassle-free living
- Feeling in control yields security
- Finding peace within yields freedom

- Discovering the flame within your heart yields respect

Use a short mantra for what you choose. For example, here is one for productivity: "Tomorrow I will wake up feeling great with high energy so I can be spiritually productive." Or, "I am 100% connected and my productivity flows."

We, the collective we, are all one and serve one God and the universe. There is no such thing as being unconnected. It is impossible. You are as connected today as you were when you were here the last time or when you were an Atlantean or an Egyptian in ancient times.

How do you find any peace when everyone is thriving on chaos and disconnection? How do you find the light when you only see darkness? Regenerate!

R	Regenerate self often
E	Entergy is depleted daily
G	Get rid of chaos and stress
E	Engage in nurturing activities
N	New thoughts & activities are part of your plan
E	Everything you think, say, feel, and do matters
R	Relax more
A	Allow time for downtime
T	Think positive thoughts
E	Every intent you set matters

Too many pre-teen and teenage children today have totally lost their way. In some cases, their parents were not involved enough in their lives to teach them or they received no moral guidance. Some of these parents were

The Second Principle: Respect

raised by adults who were part of the 60's and 70's anti-God revolution, where they believed "they" were the way. In other cases, the parents believe society owes them and therefore owes their children. The "owes them" thought process blossomed during the era of rewarding all children for participation rather than achievement. Some people have morphed that philosophy into thinking that society owes them a good job, a good income, a home, free education, etc. no matter what their abilities or accomplishments.

The answer for all is to find your inner voice and connect.

- Connect with your God and the universe.
- Connect to the power within so you can create the future you choose.
- Connect to the power within so you can overcome anything standing in your way.

The power is within. As above, so below; as without, so within; as understanding grows, so does your spiritual strength and power grow.

You are not a mistake. If you do not or cannot believe this, you have not found your respect for self. You are a physical or human expression of God's love. All humans are that expression but few show it and even fewer act upon it. Understanding that you are not a mistake but rather an expression of God's love is your strength, 100% respect for self, and the best option for success in this very moment. When you understand and live this, in this moment, you can catch a star, hitch a ride on a space ship, or find yourself peering at the pyramids.

If you are struggling way too much on your journey, relax, just let it flow. **Question much less with your ego, and trust much more with your heart**. If you want fulfilling relationships with others, use words like "equal" relationships, "fulfilling" relationships, and "loving" relationships; those are truth-filled, honest relationships. This is why truth, respect, and wisdom are so important.

When you are at peace, you will find the light. When you find the light, your truth will expand. If it is your intent to find truth and live a life filled with love and light, it will happen. Because you have found your respect you will be able to think clearly to accomplish whatever you choose. Set your intent daily; it is critical for you to accomplish all that lies in front of you. Intent is the key to reaching all goals, known and unknown.

Your ego and the outside world will try to imprison your intent and inner flame, but they cannot surpass God's love, truth, and wisdom, nor your respect for that connection. When you use love, truth, respect, and wisdom as your filters, you are living as a spiritual being. All is good, all is well, and all will turn out well.

What is missing in today's world is the ancient connecting link knowing that God is all there is. Yes, you are having a physical human experience, but what your life is all about is your spirituality. Your reason for being here in a human body is all about your spiritual work and destiny performed on Earth while in a human body. It all begins with respecting yourself and grows rapidly like a wildfire to respecting all.

The Second Principle: Respect

Chapter 7
The Third Principle: Honor All

We are human beings, but as you've been discovering, we are also are spiritual beings. Through my years of study and writing, I've discovered that we, humanity, are actually spiritual beings living in a human body, not the other way around. For centuries, perhaps millennia, we have been taught that we are the opposite: humans with occasional spiritual experiences. If you reflect upon life, look for the light and love within, you will discover the truth—that we are spiritual beings having a human experience. It takes courage to revisit your thinking about who you are—about who we are as humanity. We, like all living things, carry a vibrational energy that attracts like things and like beings.

On the surface, it may appear that we are only humans, but self-experience will quickly reveal that there are other aspects to humanity besides working, eating, and sleeping, such as fulfilling the spiritual part of us. In fact, many eastern cultures believe in an ordered life, a spiritual tradition, a way of life that yields to harmony with nature as well as others, which I refer to as "the Divine way of the universe."

Eastern philosophies/beliefs share common ground with a lifestyle filled with morality, meditation, wisdom teachings, and respect for the cardinal and intermittent directions on planet earth. This also includes up and down. Up energy, that which rises upward from the earth, is yin energy. Down energy, that which flows down from the heavens or the universe, is yang energy. They share this wisdom concept of respecting all things, directions, humans, animals, birds, plants, nature, and the universe with Native Americans and aboriginal tribes.

It became obvious that HONOR ALL was an ancient, universal principle found in almost all cultures, philosophies, religions, and societies. This principle builds upon the principle RESPECT ALL, which calls for humans to treat each other as they wish to be treated at all levels of humanity, including self, babies, children, husbands, wives, seniors, neighbors, friends, and enemies.

The significant difference is that HONOR ALL is greatly expanded to include animals, plants, trees, foul, water, land, and the air—basically, our entire environment, where we live and beyond.

The Third Principle: Honor All

UNIVERSAL TRUTH #13
PLANET EARTH HAD PERFECT BALANCE, HARMONY, HOPY, PEACE, AND JOY WHEN IT WAS CREATED.

We need to give consideration to honoring ancient philosophies that spoke of the natural cycles of planet Earth, such as weather patterns, oceanic tide cycles, and astrological cycles. For example, scientists have known for years that the Sahara Desert was once a flourishing oasis, that baby mammoths were once alive eating tropical vegetation in Siberia, and the most recent discoveries show that Antarctica once had plant life. Everything has vibrational energy cycles including our planet and humanity.

It is time to merge western and eastern philosophies that contain universal wisdom so humanity can move forward in peace and harmony, not only with each other, but with all living things. While the industrial revolution and age of technology brought us many revelations, a much softer lifestyle, and vast knowledge (even of the past), they also led to gross materialism, the squandering of precious resources, and selfishness. These are just a few examples of rhythmic cyclical time, not linear time.

THE POWER OF TIME

Time is part of this rhythmical movement and is the secret to being free of the unknown. Time reveals knowledge and wisdom, which leads to truth. Just as time continues to march on, truth continues to grow and expand, ultimately revealing more truth. For example, people once believed that the Earth was flat based on the truth known at that time. But that truth expanded when explorers discovered the surface of the earth was round. Or, just a few centuries ago, people thought the Milky Way was the universe. As we became more technologically advanced, the truth expanded and we realized that there is a vast universe beyond our Milky Way.

One truth we know is that time exists. In fact, in order for eternal thought to exist, there must be time. Time is the force that holds everything together in its space and proper place. The universe is order extended to all space, constantly moving in harmony. There is nothing to fear. Fear is darkness; light is freedom. By the Divine's thought you are a light being; therefore, avoid any darkness to prevent fear.

According to Floyd Red Crow Westerman and the Hopi Native American Prophecy, "Everything is spiritual, everything has a spirit, everything was brought here by the Creator, the One Creator. Some people call him God, some people call him Buddha, some people call him Allah, some people call him other names. We call him Tunkaschila … Grandfather. Our DNA is made out of the same DNA as the tree, the tree breathes what we exhale, we need what the tree exhales. So, we have a common destiny with the tree. You should treat all things as spirit, realize that we are one family."

They believe in being connected to everything on planet Earth. They believe in spirit God in the heavens. They believe there are cycles, such as a time to sow, a time

The Third Principle: Honor All

to reap, a time to be young and learn, and a time to be old and wise.

Time is the mechanism for creating order and calm. Staying in the chaos and disorder prevents you from entering the light. Step out of the darkness and stay in the light. Letting go or getting rid of the chaos and disorder in your life allows you time and space to create calm and harmony, which is the basis for honoring all in the universe. Calm and harmony allow the truth to enter. TODAY, today is that day.

Looking Within embodies a contemporary version of ancient truth and wisdom of honoring all that captivates the masses whether through words, feelings, music, and visually through artwork. It is about living a spiritual life where honoring all is the norm while on Earth so you can transition into a permanent spiritual world in the afterlife and be part of the majestic magnificent world of eternal peace and joy.

CONNECT TO YOUR INTENT

CONNECT! Connect with God and the universe. There is great joy and peace in knowing you are plugged in to the greatest power, the universe, your Creator, the heavens above.

- Connect to the power within so your thoughts can be received with clarity.
- Connect to the power within so you can create the future you choose.
- Connect to the power within so you can overcome anything standing in your way.
- Connect to the power within so you can honor all.

- Connect to the power within so you can maintain your spiritual continuity.
- Connect to the power within so you can find hope, peace, and joy.

Many people don't realize the connection between their thoughts, actions, and outcomes. Self-responsibility for many is non-existent. This is why honoring self, others, and all is so important. Consider this:

- If you are in a bad relationship, you need to change it by either improving it or getting out of it.
- If you are in a bad job scenario, quit wallowing in pity and victimhood and find a better job.
- If you are being compromised or abused, get out of the situation (ask for help if you need it); you deserve better.
- If you can't find a job, the answer isn't to stop trying. The answer is to either change your attitude, change the way you look for a job, and/or change where you look.
- If you see injustice or see someone harming others or animals, speak up or get help.

The list goes on and on. Set your intent and take action.

In order to change, you need to be diligent about setting your intent. Your performance directly relates to your intent for the day, the project, or the way you spend your next hour. IT'S BEST TO SET YOUR INTENT THE NIGHT BEFORE so your subconscious mind can create

The Third Principle: Honor All

your intent for the next day based on your direction or instructions.

- Before setting your intent, look back at your day to see what you accomplished yesterday. Today you can begin anew.
- Set your intent for tomorrow even if it is only one thing you seek to accomplish. You will accomplish that one thing and feel good about yourself.
- Look at what you've accomplished each day to see if it is in alignment with your mental and spiritual goals. If not, re-set your goals or re-set your "will-do" list.

Setting your intent the night before is vital. When too many days pass without setting your intent the night before, you will become confused, productivity will go down, and your focus will become distracted. Setting your intent nightly is critical for accomplishing all that lies ahead. Intent is key to reaching all goals, both known and unknown. When your accomplishments do not match your goals, you become discordant and out of balance, so you turn to mind-numbing activities that are only distracting. **Intent sets focus. Focus yields success.**

Setting intent is important because it determines how your day flows and unfolds. It determines how well you will succeed ... or not.

I	Involve yourself 100%
N	Now is the time to take charge
T	Take a step; none are wrong
E	Envision the result
N	No thoughts are irrelevant
T	Today is what matters

Intent is no minor undertaking, especially when dealing with macro concepts such as wisdom, respect, and honoring all. You accomplish all through intent, whether it is an organized thoughtful intent or an out-of-character, spur of the moment, uncontrolled emotional intent. Everything happens because of intent; even heinous crimes are the result of intent. Setting your intent is very powerful and should not be overlooked as a silent tool on the road to success and to honoring all.

Once you've set your intent, you need to control your thoughts. What you think creates your future. Focus your thoughts only on what you want to create. Be clear with your intent. Seek clarity. It is the tangible result you seek of what you believe to be truth.

C	Connect intent with results
L	Leave other thoughts and things behind
A	Accomplish your intent daily
R	Rest as needed
I	Invoke flexibility
T	Tune into yourself for awareness
Y	You can do it

Intent with clarity is a strong tool; use it wisely and daily to accomplish all that you seek.

The Third Principle: Honor All

Honor Your Journey

Looking Within encourages humanity to communicate, connect, and change the way people think about and live their life. The objective is to take what is and move it to what will best serve you, humanity, the planet, and the universe. Everything is connected. Nothing stands alone. All is one, one is all. When the vibrational energy of one changes, it affects the all.

Think three. Three is the master's key to unlocking everything. Three is the number of creation. The famous inventor Nikola Tesla once said, "If you only knew the magnificence of the numbers 3, 6, and 9, then you would have the key to the universe." Think of the Trinity in Christianity. Think of the saying, "As above, so below, and so within." Three is the key to whatever challenges you. There are always three steps, three things, or three issues involved. **For example:**

- You put two things together and you create three.
- When you create a painting, you put together your idea and your knowledge of painting, apply the paint to the canvas, and the third thing is the completed canvas.
- When you write a book, you take the ideas in your head, put them on paper, and once you've added a publisher you have the third item, a book.
- When two people unite in marriage, those two united people create a third entity, a family.

Another example is planet Earth. If you don't have the moon and the sun, planet Earth would not stay in its fixed position and would no longer exist. Three is the foundational formula, the glue that holds the universe together and also expands the universe.

The concept of three works wonderfully with the Honor All principle: First, you use your wisdom and honor your Creator by your connection. Second, you honor yourself by finding your flame within, you became mind, body, and spirit. Third, you honor all else, humanity, the environment and the Creator. The knowledge and wisdom of three is the key to the universe, both within and without or above and below.

Here's another example. To create wellbeing, you need to use three steps; three is the key to good health.

1. Determine what you want good health to look like.
2. Determine what needs to change.
3. Takes the necessary steps to accomplish your new good health.

Choose feeling great over feeling okay. Choose living over existing. You are not here to exist, but rather to find and give great joy, peace, and understanding.

This is the time to make dramatic change. You can when you use three simple steps.

- Remove things that no longer serve you well.
- Release things that are standing in your way.
- Regenerate self to full energy vibration so you can attract better vibrational energy in your life.

Every human comes to planet Earth with a purpose for being, above and beyond what they choose to make

The Third Principle: Honor All

of life. Many create a life that is the polar opposite of their spiritual destiny agreement, making it very difficult during youth and early adulthood to see a spiritual destiny that may or may not be compatible.

If you're struggling, or if you're having difficulty honoring all, it's time to regenerate! Are you running on empty? Are you overworked, over-stressed, anxious, and tired? You are absolutely in need of re-fueling, regenerating, and re-invigorating. This is a sign that your vibrational energy is running on fumes. In this state it is almost impossible to honor yourself, much less to honor others or all. When you're surrounded by chaos and going through significant change, it is important to regenerate yourself often—sometimes weekly, other times daily. You cannot go full speed ahead 100% of the time 24/7 in the human world.

When you are out of control of even a small part of your life, it disrupts all parts of your life and you no longer perform well or feel well. This is a big problem in most people's lives. They don't understand that when the little things go out of control, big things fall apart too. When little things go uncorrected, big things become chaotic. That's why it is important that you feed and nurture yourself and get ample rest.

Truth and wisdom are your journey. They are your path, your life commitment, and your agreement for coming here. Jesus is not the one to worship. He is not the one for adoration or the one to connect to. It is God, our Creator, the Divine. Jesus came to point the way to God, to pray to God, to acknowledge that God's way, the Divine Kingdom, will be the same on Earth as it is in heaven. Your job is to realize this and help bring heaven to Earth. The spiritual rules for living are key to everlasting peace, harmony, and joy.

Honor Heaven

How do you find truth in a sea of darkness?

Truth speaks boldly, with conviction and an empowered, unrelenting compassion of the need for spiritual reconnection. In order to survive through the next several decades, people will need to put on a shield of truth—truth that leads to a spiritual connectedness to God and the universe. The ultimate goal is a 100% connection to God and the universe 100% of the time, which leads to peace, calm, and an understanding of the deep internal heart/Creator connection within. It is with this heart/Creator connection that humanity can honor all.

So, the question remains, how do you survive when the world is disintegrating?

- How do you face tomorrow when you have lost everything today?
- How do you find light when you only see darkness?
- How do you create a better tomorrow when everything you believe is being destroyed?
- How do you connect with others when they think a connection is electronic, not at the heart level?
- How do you find any peace when everyone is thriving on chaos and disconnection?
- How do you find truth in an ocean of darkness and chaos?

The Third Principle: Honor All

Yes, the message is the same as in ancient times, but for a different millennium and a different set of inhabitants of the world and planet. The original message was in ancient Egypt where Osiris was their Immaculate Conception, and Isis the Virgin Mary. Then came the millennium that began the last 2,000 years with Jesus born to a whole new generation of humanity filled with new rulers, new dogma, and new societal rules.

The Spiritual learning curve put forth here is to:

1. Make meditation part of your daily routine. Adopt Gandhi's philosophy, "It's going to be a busy day. I need to meditate twice as long."
2. Become who you have always been, a spiritual being having a human experience.
3. Use your gifts of creativity, writing, painting, speaking, and mindfulness to serve others and the universe.
4. Create a message for wisdom, knowledge, and ancient ways for humanity to come together.
5. Give humanity a new understanding of what humanity is, how it should reorder its life to thrive in the new mindfulness world, and how to make that transformation.

Heaven is a place of eternal energy. It is the home of all that is good, all that is pure, all that is.

Heaven is a place of harmony, balance, and flowing energy, not what the common understanding of what it is. While human beings who meet on Earth in any given lifetime may meet again in heaven, that is not the purpose of heaven and such encounters will be by design, not chance. Create your own heaven on Earth filled with hope, peace and joy by taking control of your life and honoring all so you can create the future you want. Only then will humanity get past their anger and pain, and build a bridge to the future.

The Energy of Connection and Honor

Everything is connected in perfect vibrational harmony, because everything *is* vibrational energy. We are vibrational beings. Therefore, when you show up, know who shows up. Look inside your own being to see where you are off. Come to terms with your own being. Life wants to harmonize, to be in alignment. Be a passionate magnet. Get rid of the old. Love raises vibration; fear lowers frequencies.

Thoughts create results. Think wisely and carefully so you can create what you want, not what you don't want. You can use a mantra as follows: "I choose to surround myself with my 100% connection to God and the universe. Together we will honor all and thrive."

Transform or transcend your self-imposed limitations. It is through consciousness and spirituality that you become who you are meant to be. So be passionate about the possibilities of what could be. From nowhere comes something—something that can be molded and shaped into something of great value to self, humanity, and the universe.

Think about your own experiences. At a spiritual session, meeting, or service, are you bored or maybe not getting enjoyment out of it? Maybe the music is good? Maybe it's not so good? Is that a reason to go or not go? Do you attend and expect to enjoy it and be entertained?

The Third Principle: Honor All

Or something else? Are you expecting to get something in return?

Do you feel judged by yourself or others? Do you wonder if you're not doing things a certain way or the right way? Do those things have anything to do with how you relate to God or your personal connection with God? Do you come away feeling like you're not adequate.? Do you often say things like, "I'm not good enough," or "I'm not doing things the right way"? Often, when you go home and really think about it, the two things are not even related.

The increasing awareness of a higher consciousness or the direct connection to God and the universe is spirituality.

The Divine Way today is through a direct connection to God and the universe. You have a direct line to the universe. God and the universe are open 24/7 for communication and connection, and when you still and silence your mind, you will hear the response.

The way you know you are communicating with the Divine is by these qualifications:

1. The response is in your best interest.
2. The response bears no ill will to others, and brings no harm to others.
3. The response leaves your world, no matter how large or small, in a better place.

Look for the goodness in things or the darkness in things. Seek the light, diminish the darkness. The Divine Way is about helping humanity move forward to creating a better, more peaceful world. You are an essential contributor to this forward movement.

Create! Remember that there are many ways to open one's heart and honor all besides reading this book. Being creative, whether that's through writing, painting, sculpting, dancing, photography, or anything else, is important during all phases of the journey. That's one of the reasons for the explosion of art during the Renaissance of the Middle Ages. It's time for our second Renaissance of Joy.

So make good use of your time today. It is one less day you have on planet Earth. Don't worry about yesterday. Focus on today. And remember, be flexible like the palm tree. In a storm a palm tree may sway and even lose all its fronds, but it stands strong to live another day. All things will unfold as planned.

Societies were meant to live in harmony with each other and nature. They are to honor all, care for and protect each other, nurture when needed, guide when necessary, but above all love one another as they love themselves.

Honor all things so the planet with all its life forms can thrive. Out there is not some distant void, but rather the macro of the micro within.

Positive vibrational energy flows and has a special place in your life. All things need to flow around you, through you, or to you for you to be in balance.

The Third Principle: Honor All

Honor All leads to Harmony.

Chapter 8
The Fourth Principle: Equality

Begin a new day in reflection of the universe, the world, your life, and your personal circle. We as individuals and families are having typical experiences where relationships are disconnected and disjointed, resulting in us not looking out for each other—family members, neighbors, and community members.

Today, it's all about ego: selfishness, self-centeredness, and self-indulgence. But there is hope because there are patches of people in every community who are energetically holding together their families, their neighbors, and the community. These patches of people act as an interconnected grid around the world that is keeping in place the foundational energy needed so humanity can catch up and start expanding that beautiful cohesive grid into one solid beautiful mass of love and light.

Looking Within

Humanity is at one of its darkest points in modern history and will continue to decline unless positive change in macro proportions occurs. This change must bubble up from within. It cannot be found in electronics, social media platforms, materialism, or in any of the self-serving totalitarian groups popping up online and around the world.

To find the answers, to find the truth, one must go inward and search the heart until the truth is found. Remember the old adage, "Seek and you will find." What your energy focuses on is what you will receive. If you seek truth within, you will find it. If you seek it without, you may find bits and pieces of it hidden within the darkness, but you also risk finding only the darkness.

UNIVERSAL TRUTH #14
CONNECTING WITHIN HELPS CREATE
BETTER LIFE EXPERIENCES AND
PROVIDES YOU DIRECTION.

Make time every day to go within and seek the truth. You will find what you seek—TRUTH—the truth of the universe, light, and love. That truth will lead you to universal correspondence, or EQUALITY.

In a society where a deep abiding eternal connection is frowned upon, inequality, discrimination, corruption, and chaos thrive, growing uncontrollably like a massive wild fire. It takes living by the previously discussed principles in this book to wake up and realize that EQUALITY must be the next principle.

The Fourth Principle: Equality

RECLAIM YOUR GIFTS

Humanity was a gift to planet Earth by the Creator, the One. Humanity came with equality hardwired into its DNA. It wasn't something we had to seek out. It wasn't something hard to understand. Equality was a gift from the Divine. Each individual was to be respected by all—to have equality.

But over time, things didn't go as planned. As the stronger sought wealth and control, the weak were overrun and cannibalized into a mere likeness of humanity, unable to protect themselves. Their freedom of speech was shattered. Their wellbeing was sliced and diced until they had no will left but just to survive. This is where we are today. Even in nations that purport to be freedom-based, we are not really free.

For example, it is no longer safe to express your personal, political, or religious opinions without fear of being emotionally and sometimes physically accosted by radical groups that believe their way is the only way. It is not safe to walk in certain neighborhoods or shop in certain areas depending on your ethnic or racial background. We are no longer free to go to a nightclub or a concert without wondering if we will make it out alive. In a court of law, we are no longer guaranteed a fair trial due to prejudice on the part of jurors and even the seated magistrate.

Today it's all about conquer and divide, tear down history, demoralize, re-educate, and control. It's about deception, a constant false narrative, betrayal, social engineering the narrative, and keeping us divided. This is an alien world compared to what is hardwired into our DNA and expected by the Divine Way of living.

Equality is about accepting our diversity. It's also about focusing on our commonality rather than our differences. It's not about whether one is rich and the other is poor, or one drives a car and the other doesn't. It is about the person, the individual you connect with at the heart level. One person should never have to ride in the back of the bus because another says so. This is why we are building a bridge to a new way of life where all of humanity is equal with equally important roles to play while on planet Earth. Again, I'm talking about the role you agreed to perform spiritually during this lifetime.

It is time to move forward to a Divine Way of life. We are a society in great need of the wisdom and truth of the ancient civilizations. Our current reality will never thrive if it continues on its current path. It is time for individuals to be able to live at their fullest potential. Only then can we cross the bridge from where we are to a new world of unadulterated, unhindered EQUALITY.

Connect—connect with our Creator. Connect with each other so the truth can flow, so it can escape the dungeon of doubt, fear, and half-truths. It takes you, me, all of us to expose the half-truths as lies so freedom can be free of the shackles placed on it.

Truth will be shackled and hidden no more. Humanity, the universe, and our Creator are insisting that **now is the time to awaken, transform, and be enlightened**. There are no more tomorrows left. The time for truth, wisdom, equality, and enlightenment has been revealed. It is now!

The Fourth Principle: Equality

It is time for each of us to take that first step onto our path, to begin our journey. There is no fear of failure; our still and calm inner voice will guide us through easy and difficult times. Share your awesomeness with the world so all may grow as all of humanity awakens from their deep sleep to remember who they are.

The day you were born does matter. Built into your birth date is your direct connection to our Creator, your destiny, your spiritual commitment, and your life journey on planet Earth. Your date of birth creates your astrological roadmap, which is often overlooked in modern society, but was openly visible to the three wiseman at Christ's birth.

Your astrological sign tells you who you are, where you've been, and what lies ahead. While you are in control and have the freedom of choice, destiny is written in the stars. The location of the stars when you are born is your roadmap to your future and will take you where you need to go. There is no one else on planet Earth or in the universe like you. There is no one else who can do what you do, be creative like you, and deliver the message you have. Create your own heaven on Earth filled with peace and joy by taking control of your life so you can create the future you want. Be the person you were meant to be.

BE THE CHANGE

Bringing heaven to Earth is an important lifestyle change for our planet because with this change comes equality. While you can create a balanced, chaos-free physical environment based on Feng Shui principles, it is but one step. It is not enough to really enjoy a full, stress-free, prosperous life in the twenty-first century and beyond. It takes more to offset our self-imposed, overscheduled lifestyle filled with cement cities, noise pollution, and chaos. It takes so much more. The fears we generate or are forced upon us are too many and we can't compensate for the self-imposed, anxious world in which we have imprisoned ourselves.

During this time of great anxiety, it's important to focus on direct contact, thoughts, feelings, and actions that come from our God, our First Source, our Creator, and spiritual guides. It is important that you change your way of life now so you can be free from human/ego thinking and fill your entire self with nothing but unadulterated contact, thought, feelings, and actions that come from God or your inner self, your guides, and the universe. The only way you can bring heaven to Earth and create equality is to make this shift.

Every human wants to be unconditionally loved, respected, and treated equally. Every human wants to live in harmony without strife. Every human wants peace within and to know they are safe. The world is void and vacant of feeling; there is no heaven ever coming to Earth if we continue on the path we are currently on. The world is filled with chaos, inequality, fear, and hatred, and is teaching future generations more fear, inequality, chaos, and hatred. Your voice is needed! People are waiting to hear it. Many are actively seeking it but know not where to find it. Truth overcomes obstacles. Truth always wins out. Truth has power in its name and cannot be overcome, torn down, or defeated. Truth energizes equality.

Be Who You Are

Be who you are
not what others want you to be.
Be who you are
that's who you were destined to be.
Be who you are
you have much work ahead.
Be who you are
your work will provide hope.
Be who you are
your words will be inspiring.
Be who you are
your world is on fire.
Be who you are
the time has arrived.
Be who you are
the world awaits you.
Be who you are
there was no one else.
Be who you are
your success is already written.

The ultimate goal is 100% connection to God and the universe 100% of the time, which will lead to peace, calm, and understanding on the deep internal soul connection level within. The more people who connect with the Creator, the One, First Source and with each other, the faster the world will change for the better. Your spiritual connection and truth with wisdom applied is the great equalizer.

Lift your eyes upward and see the light. The energy is in the light but the darkness hides the light. Stay in the light mentally, emotionally, and physically. You cannot go where there is all darkness and thrive.

Lift up your eyes so you can feel. Open your heart so you can see. Listen so you can be. All is within. Bring it without so you can be productive and receive the maximum benefit of your ancient wisdom and knowledge.

Quiet your mind so you can hear; close your eyes so you can see.

The collective we is charged with helping humanity get past their anger and pain so we can build a bridge to a better future. Tomorrow is here. We must provide the physical earthly tools for the universe to move everything forward.

Focus is the key to all one does. Focus is the key to all you accomplish. Focus is the answer you seek.

Human life today is disposable, not what was intended by God and the universe. Human life is a gift, something to be honored and treasured, but in many areas of the world life is destroyed before it is born. Young lives are destroyed by hate before they grow up, and female lives are battered and bruised and mutilated. The undesired are killed and maimed; some are destroyed by words only, others by deception. This is not equality.

Humans were created to love and nurture each other, treat each other equally, and stay connected with God and the universe. They may have become self-absorbed,

The Fourth Principle: Equality

self-adulated, and void of feelings or connections. There is a vast emptiness that will be filled by others that is not necessarily in the best interest of humanity, or it will be filled by ancient wisdom and truth.

These ancient wisdoms and truth can guarantee success. Lacking them will lead to minimum or poor performance, and worst-case scenario, failure.

There is no "them" versus "us," no universe versus humanity, and no God versus man. That is all a myth. We are all one, with no separate parts. Your human experience is also that of a spiritual or universe experience. What happens out there is also happening within you and every human. That is correspondence or connection or equality. Out there is not some distant void but rather the macro, the universe of the micro within, the universe within our body. It is all within, always has been and always will be. You are what your soul/heart has always been; all your knowledge within is of the universe without. There is no "them" versus "us."

Wisdom, commitment, and discernment are alarmingly absent in the world today, whether in the home, in relationships, or in the workplace. Knowing what is important and moving in that direction at all times is commitment, being flexible when interruptions are important enough to move your focus elsewhere is discernment, and wisdom is knowing what should take precedence. These attributes are the key to being fully engaged, maximizing focus, and creating an environment conducive to success. By applying these principles to your personal life and incorporating them into your leadership skills, you will reduce chaos, distractions, and stress while dramatically increasing equality, productivity, performance, and sustainability.

The goal for each human is to remember first that they are a spiritual being having a human experience. For the fulfillment of their experience, they need to re-find their eternal connection to God and the universe. Through this they will find their destiny.

This is the overriding message about living a better more fulfilling human life.

What did you come here to do? What is your destined way to serve humanity? Whether it is discovering the theory of relativity or creating advanced technology such as smart phones, we each have one unique thing to do that is ours and ours alone.

Silence your mind and you will find your voice. Control your thoughts and you will become who you are.

How do you create a better tomorrow when everything you believe in is being destroyed today? Think, "I am filled with God's love. I am love. I am truth. I am created equal. I am wisdom." How would equality, love, truth, and wisdom act or respond in any set of circumstances?

How do you face tomorrow when you've lost everything today? You need to know that you are always cradled in the arms of God, the Creator.

FOOD FOR THOUGHT

Tall and short palm trees represent life, the flow of life, and constant change. With each new branch, each wind, each circumstance it ever changes, but it bends and flows with the tides of change. This is part of self-improvement.

The Fourth Principle: Equality

But don't miss the important steps for improvement, which include reading, reflection, and regeneration.

All is good that is coming—endings of the old and beginnings of the NEW including the activation of equality.

Stop! Stop beating yourself up. You have much on your mind and lots to do. Most of us expect too much of ourselves and plan too little. Focus on your intent.

Life is about eternity, not just today. Today will take care of itself if you take care of eternity. Change your focus and you will change your result. Everything is connected 100% of the time. Out of chaos we can move into clarity as long as we are connected and practicing equality. Follow the light, be one with the light, and you will experience peace.

Your heart is eternally connected for infinity. You are never disconnected. You cannot ever disconnect. You can ignore, not acknowledge, or be disconnected from your perspective, but you are always tethered to God and the universe, God's love, God's goodness, God's eternal presence.

Today

Today is important; what did you do?
Today is the present; are you focused?
Today is the NOW; did you notice today is why you are alive. Did you recognize it?
Today is the only day you can live in this moment.
Today is why you are here; don't miss it.

There are five stages to soul/heart growth. Those five spiritual stages are:

1. Hopefulness: find the above and below connection.
2. Spirituality: the increasing awareness of a higher consciousness.
3. Wisdom: creating harmony from chaos.
4. Transcending: moving beyond your self-imposed limitations.
5. Consciousness: knowing that I Am (for a review of "I AM," reread chapter 5).

Move through life with the curves; energy and cycles flow; the angles are barriers and chaos.

It is written in the stars that change is coming. It will be a new way of living, a new lifestyle with appreciation for life, others, and everything in your surroundings.

Listen for the still voice within and you will always hear.
Listen for the still voice within and you will know.
Listen for the still voice within and you will be wise.
Listen for the still voice within and you will hear the truth.
Listen for the still voice within and equality will become reality.

Time is truth. It is now.

The Fourth Principle: Equality

Chapter 9
The Fifth Principle:
Self-Control

Peace is not always easy to define, but for most it may include some of the following:

- A quiet place to live and safely raise a family
- Financial security
- Free speech
- Neighborhood safety
- Freedom to worship where and when they wish
- Equality
- Respect
- Freedom from control by others including governments
- Freedom to live life as they choose as long as it brings no harm to others

This list could differ greatly from person to person, location to location, or culture to culture. But the one thing that would be on everyone's list would be the right to live and die with respect and dignity. Whether upper, middle, or lower class as defined financially by the government, everyone wants to be acknowledged for their contribution to life and be appreciated as a human being.

When you're young, you feel like you can conquer the world until somebody bigger or more important than you, or the government, stands in your way. It is that moment in time that defines you. This defining moment may happen at age 10 or 27, but happen it will. It can happen later in life, though it is not as common. Some never grow up to be adults emotionally and especially spiritually. They may hover at 13 or 23 emotionally all their lives. It is also at one of these points that a person usually begins their journey within as they search for something, anything, to make their life more worthwhile and meaningful. This is when many people take their first step toward exploring the concept of self-control.

As for me, even though I never felt disconnected from my Creator, God, the Divine, I didn't start to grasp the importance of something more important in life until I was 29. And it was at least 25 years later when I really got the message and started my journey within. That was when I noticed the cyclical nature of my life and started asking questions like, "Why does this keep happening to me?"

The day I asked the question, "What career path should I follow?" I was shocked by the answer, which became my wakeup call. The answer was and still is my definition of my career.

Career

Mustering the courage
to honor, recognize, accept and display
the truth of who I am
every given millisecond
through non-judgment,
having the willingness
to re-organize and re-center.

This statement defined not only my career but it also defines everyone's career.

As a reminder, career isn't about what you do on planet Earth. It is about who you are and what you came here to do as part of humanity. It isn't about fancy cars, an expensive home, or a country club lifestyle. It isn't about taking drugs, the latest techno gadgets, how many followers you have on social media, or who can get the latest version of a smart phone first.

It's about your spiritual work while on planet Earth. It's about you, me, and what we are at the core. It's about moving beyond each cycle so you can progress on your journey, not continually relive the current cycle you are on and repeat the same mistakes.

It's about what's on the inside of you that needs to come out so you can help the world be a better place to live. It's about whether you will be the one to invent the next vaccine to save millions of lives or help an elderly person safely cross a street. Only you are accountable for who you are and how you impact the world.

Who knows how many new Mozarts, Gershwins or John Williams are out there spending time on mindless keyboards or playing video games while the artistry of their music is lost to antiquity? Will you be the next Monet, Rembrandt, Mikhail Baryshnikov, Babe Ruth, Shaquille O'Neal, Steve Jobs, Malala Yousafzai, Tom Clancy, or Jane Austin?

Who are you on the inside? If you don't know, what are you going to do to find out? It's time to discover what your "career" is and why you came to planet Earth. Be you! Be the person you were born to be.

Focus on Self

There is a renaissance coming, a new swing of the pendulum, and humanity awaits its creative entrance into the world. What will you be known for once you are gone? Being a good son, daughter, spouse, co-worker, or boss isn't all you were born to do on planet Earth. Look within and find the truth.

Everything you think, say, feel, and do matters because that is how you create your future. Yes, re-read that. EVERYTHING you are or have is the result of your thoughts, feelings, words, and actions in your past—anytime from the last few minutes to five years ago to a decade ago. If you keep doing the same things the same way, the result will be the same and you will start your old cycle anew.

The Fifth Principle: Self-Control

UNIVERSAL TRUTH #15
EVERYTHING YOU THINK, SAY, FEEL, AND DO MATTERS BECAUSE THAT IS HOW YOU CREATE YOUR FUTURE.

YOU are in control of your life! The problem is that for the first several years of your life you are filled with other humans' and society's knowledge, prejudices, rules, and opinions. This makes you a conglomeration of all their thinking long before you are old enough to think on your own and become the person you were born to be. Instead you become what everyone else thinks you should be. You are expected to conform to those thoughts, prejudices, and information that all those in control have forced upon you. This leads us to the principle of SELF-CONTROL.

In a world where chaos yields fear, anxiety, and despondence, it is easy to become jaded and let others take control. We are up against a series of assumptions implanted by our family, culture, government, religion, and society. Collectively they have taught us that everything is out of our control and that we have no responsibility or accountability for our thoughts and actions. They teach us that all our bad decisions and outcomes are because of someone or something else. This gives birth to a victimhood society that welcomes someone else being in control.

STOP! Everything is *not* out of your control and does not depend on someone or something else. That is simply not true. Just as I am in control of my thoughts and actions, you too are in control of you, your thoughts, and your actions. It is up to all of us to sift through the years and years of other's input until you find the truth, the universe's truth, ancient wisdom.

Your thoughts create your personal life, the microcosm of the world you live in, the people you choose to have or not have in your life, your actions, words, and feelings. Choose wisely because you are creating your future, be it good or bad, inconsequential or meaningful.

You are the only you there is. No other person has come to Earth to be who you are and what you are supposed to be. It is written in your DNA what role you are to play while on Earth. Are you going to follow those in control and create a living hell filled with hate and darkness? Or are you going to follow the Divine Way of helping others and yourself find a better way of life filled with hope, peace, joy, and connection?

It truly is your choice. You weren't ordered to do so but rather made a commitment upon entering Earth. Humanity needs you to get in control of your life so you can help move spirituality and humanity forward. This is an inner knowingness that you find when seeking truth and justice, and honoring all. One is not separate from the other. All are one and one is all.

Native American Lakota wisdom sheds great light on humanity and the importance of the individual. It's all about how to conduct self and what is expected of the individual human on Earth.

The Circle

> In the circle we are all equal
> There is no one in front of you
> There is no one behind you
> There is no one above you
> There is no one below you
> The circle is sacred because it is
> Designed to create unity
>
> -Native American Lakota Wisdom

This is the perfect description of self, how to respect others, and how to become a selfless, in-control part of humanity—one that contributes positively to the future wellbeing of our world. It isn't just about us, the lower case us, but US, the whole, the masses.

The Lakota further believe that minds and bodies do get corrupted and need healing, as do feelings and emotions. They ask their Creator, the Healer, to heal them and they look to their spirit guides, helpers, and ancestors for guidance.

Within the circle is a lot of power as it represents the individual, the family, the community, and the nation. That power is a little like throwing a pebble into a pond and watching the ripples spread outward, overtaking whatever they come in contact with. If there is no self-control in the center, the negative influence on all it touches magnifies and creates great instability and disharmony. If there is self-control, love, light, and truth in the circle, then love, light, and peace expand and thrive. One individual human can cripple or destroy a family, a community, or a nation when out of control and acting selfishly.

Self-control always begins with me and my relationship with myself. It then becomes a great example for others.

This book is about that transformation. To transform you first need to connect and understand that you are a spiritual being fulfilling a human destiny. The more complete your transformation is, the more at peace you will be. Becoming who you were meant to be brings joy. Joy is the transformation and harmonizing of your inner and outer worlds.

Basic Principles to Remember

I've spoken frequently throughout this book of the need for silence, meditation, or prayer as a way of connecting to the Divine, God, and the universe. There is one more way you might find fun and enjoyable on days where you just can't quite seem to make your connection or you can't quiet your mind—CREATIVITY.

Creativity is defined as the use of your imagination or original ideas within, especially in the production of artwork. When you leave the logical side of the brain and put your mind in a creative mood, your mind steps back and allows your inner voice to step forward and take control. That is your inner you, your Divine connection. It doesn't particularly matter what type of creativity you are doing—sculpting, writing, dancing, music, painting, knitting, weaving, crocheting etc. The very act of being

The Fifth Principle: Self-Control

creative allows the voice of the Divine to connect directly with you. If you consider the physical process involved, the creativity comes from within, and travels to your hands which are directly connected to your heart. Creativity opens your world up to connecting with the Divine just as well as meditation and prayer. The more you engage in creativity, the more self-control you will feel.

- Creativity is the natural order of life. Life is energy, pure creative energy.
- There is an underlying, in-dwelling creative force infusing all of life, including ourselves.
- When we open ourselves to our creativity, we open ourselves to the Creator's creativity within us and our lives.
- We are ourselves, creations. We, in turn, are meant to continue creativity by being creative ourselves.
- Creativity is God's gift to use. Using our creativity is our gift back to God.
- The refusal to be creative is self-will and is counter to our true nature.
- When we open ourselves to exploring our creativity, we open ourselves to God: **G**ood **O**rderly **D**irection.
- As we open our creative channel to the Creator, many gentle but powerful changes are to be expected.
- It is safe to open ourselves up to greater and greater creativity.

- Our creative dreams and yearnings come from a divine source. As we move toward our dreams, we move toward our divinity.

While *Looking Within* is in part about creating heaven on Earth, it is also about living in harmony with nature and each other. When you create order in the universe through creativity and connection, it yields peace-filled continuity on planet Earth. Order in your life provides peace-filled continuity in your life and enhances your ability to find a deep meaningful connection with your Creator and the universe and provide humanity hope and joy.

Yesterday is gone; tomorrow is here. The stars continue their march forward until they end and then they begin all over again, a new cycle. You are about staying connected 100% of the time—that's one way to describe what the Divine Way provides. Another way to describe it is to be spiritually active listening within. Either way works, but touches different hearts.

Connecting your heart is a key to both mind/heart alignment and retrieving ancient wisdom. Always approach life from a spiritual point of view. Stay focused spiritually rather than humanly, gently bring your focus back to the moment, and let your creativity blossom.

Humans over think, over plan, over work, over everything. This makes life so much more complex than needed. Consider these facts:

- The ancient wisdom of messages like the Emerald Tablets from ancient Egypt is very important and is one piece of the foundation for humanity to

move forward. Its ancient wisdom and truths are being turned into understandable modern language. It is time the masses know what the alchemists knew in medieval times.
- This ancient wisdom and truth are creating new ways for humanity to think, feel, and live their lives in greater harmony, peace, and abundance. It will bring together the western philosophy of "do unto others as you would have done to you," and a mixture of eastern philosophy based on the concept that "all truth is found within." This collective philosophy, the Divine Way, will become a new lifestyle, including the flow of energy within and without.

Your heart is where the answers lie. Your heart is where God resides. Still your mind so you can hear God's voice and your heart. Still your mind, and the way will be shown to find any answer or reach any objective. The most important thing about having a goal is having one, and then taking action.

FLOW OF ENERGY AND FOCUS

To focus your energy and enhance your self-control, consider these suggestions:

- Remove things.
- Release things.
- Regenerate Self.
- The placement of furniture yields positions of power or opportunity.

- The colors of walls should yield calm, soothing operations.
- Organization yields efficiency and effectiveness.
- Recognition of self and others yields increased productivity.
- Self-motivation yields improved creativity and sustainability.

Spirituality is the increasing awareness of a higher consciousness. An instructional word to use for this continued spirituality and creativity is the word "flow."

F	Freedom from boundaries
L	Love of what you create
O	Owning your own abilities
W	Wanting to share the joy with others

Flow has a special place in your life as it leads to self-control. All things need to flow around you, through you, or to you for you to be in balance. It's all about creating heaven on Earth in this lifetime. Some will get it and really understand that they need to take action. The principle of the Divine Way will show them how. Others will look at this work and learn what they need to do, and yet others will realize this book is sounding the alarm.

Learn, listen, feel; all is available to you. Heal yourself so you get clarity and can move forward. Listen to your heart so you can hear. Allow your heart to take you on a journey inward so you can see.

You are on a beautiful journey, a path that is yours alone. Everyone is on the path that is their own. They simply have not discovered that truth—truth that will be

The Fifth Principle: Self-Control

revealed to them. In fact, this book is revealing three truths that everyone needs to embrace:

1. Everyone has a journey, and they are somewhere on their path.
2. Everyone learns life lessons while traveling their path. They either learn their lesson or continue to repeat the experience cycle after cycle.
3. Growth on your path is eternal. New experiences lead you to growth and new truths.

There is no one else on planet Earth or in the universe that is like you. There is no one else that can do what you can do, whether it's paint artwork, sculpt, play music, create, or anything you excel at.

If you're unsure what your gifts are, this is where active spiritual listening comes into play. I first introduced Active Spiritual Listening in Chapter 6. It's worth repeating the 3 guidelines of Active Spiritual Listening here.

- Make a conscious decision to be 100% connected 100% of the time, or be an active listener to spiritual guidance at all times.
- Have an intense personal relationship with your inner thoughts, mind, and ego. Your thoughts within should be in control of you, not your mind. Your spiritual self must be in control to proceed on your journey or down your path.
- Be 100% aware of every time you and all of your thoughts move away from your spiritual being so you can return and not repeat a cycle.

It is so easy for humans to think it is all about them and their overblown egos of importance. But if one views the universe, humans are but a speck of sand whose sole purpose is to remember who they are, where they came from, and get plugged into the Source, God, or the universe.

Your present action creates your future. **You have to be the change to create your own transformation.** So, wash away the resistance to your own existence. Love is the true hidden treasure. Take the wheel; set your course; you can go anywhere.

Be! Reflect on who you've met along your journey while you've become the new you. Let it soak in. You are no longer who you were and are becoming what you were meant to be. Be the beautiful person within and without that you are. Step away from human wanderings and leave behind all that is earthly. You no longer need any of that to accomplish your destiny.

It is this quiet revolution that is going to tap into and bring about self-control and change among all humanity. People want something to ground themselves with, but it's not quite religion. It's that deep longing and yearning inside that they realize is missing, but they don't quite know how to find it, what it is, and how to get it. As new spiritual beings enter, old ones make room by leaving. This is a universal truth. There is a steady cycle of entering and leaving, a flow of energy vibration that creates life.

With your hardwired connection all is possible; nothing is impossible. In a free society, all is possible, as long as it brings no harm to others.

The Fifth Principle: Self-Control

EMBRACE YOUR TRANSFORMATION

Our job right now is to get in control of ourselves and learn how to transform self from the base level of humanity to the spiritual level. This is why it's vital to be present and to live in the moment to yield love. Living in the past is a life filled with regret, and living in the future is wishing your life away. Be all that you can be—fulfilled love. Learn to manifest perfect clients, perfect projects, perfect income, and perfect relationships—all this can afford you what you want to be provided.

Choose living over existing. You are not here to exist but find and give great joy, peace, and understanding. Many don't even realize they are hungering but they do feel an emptiness and a yearning for something. That something is TRUTH and everything that makes up Creating Heaven on Earth. Your destiny (everyone's destiny) is here and now, in the present, not the future.

Take control of your emotional feelings and you will be more productive. You cannot go where there is darkness and thrive. Let go. Let go of everything from the past. Let go of what you thought was important, the career you thought you had to have, the relationships you think you have. It is time to move into your future. Your future is in the light right in front of you, not in the past and not in the darkness.

You know that God is I AM. The simple definition of I AM is you 100% connected to God 100% of the time. Consciousness is I AM.

Do not waver; do not forget to set your INTENT every night before you fall asleep to create the tomorrow you want. Setting your intent is vital for reclaiming your self-control. Review Chapter 7 again for specifics about intent. Remember, intent plus action words are where everything begins.

Turbulence and great upheaval will continue to cause much fear and grieving on planet Earth and continue to feed the fire of the monster by consuming hope and joy and converting it to chaos and fear. That is what you are all about! You are **not** here to live your life and simply vote present. You are here to provide soulmates and humans hope for the future. Where there is hope there is no fear. Where there is light, darkness cannot exist.

You are a spiritual being having a human earthly experience. You are creating a good habit to provide empowerment. Good habits lead to a future of abundance. Good habits lead to reduced stress. Good habits result in success. The ancient wisdom and the Divine Way principles give you a roadmap on how to proceed on your journey to accomplish your complete transformation and return to your spiritual roots. The universe is a thought created by all that is, bringing with it order and harmony. Creating heaven on Earth is a desire of all humanity, no matter what color their skin or nationality or religion. Heaven on Earth is the singular goal of humanity once connected with the Divine, most just cannot articulate it.

It is all about the flow, the unending connection, the flow through that connection from the universe to each of us, and the flow from each of us to the universe. As an example, if you wish to see financial reward, use words like abundance, prosperity, joy, and wealth.

Focus on this minute, not any other. Focus on today, not tomorrow. Focus on what is at hand, not what isn't or could be, or could never be. Your strength and best option for success is this very moment. When you com-

The Fifth Principle: Self-Control

plete this moment, you can catch a star in the next moment or hitch a ride on a space ship, stand beside the pyramids, or be with the hundreds of other ancient civilizations that existed on planet Earth before us.

Planet Earth is parched and barren when it comes to compassion, concern, and connection. There is a systematic breakdown within society where no one is accountable to anyone, including themselves. Few really believe in God and a connection to the universe, even fewer believe that there truly is a divine order to everything.

There is great order in the universe. The universe cannot exist in chaos, nor can a human. Self-control is vital. The more you allow outside thinking inside, the more chaos is created. The deeper you go within, the fewer cycles you will repeat, and you will create more hope, peace, joy, love, and light.

Chapter 10
The Sixth Principle: Truth

Words have power to open doors for the heart within; within lies the power to above and below.

The arts, science, and religion were supposed to be the three equal systems of a unified social order depicting truth and reality. In the 21st century, only one of these three equivalent aspects of truth or reality—science—is said to have relevancy. In fact, since the scientific revolution in the 16th and 17th centuries, art and religion were relegated to the back of the room and given little or no weight in societal values and depicting the truth. With the massive advancement of technology, science continues to have a choke hold on any advancement of the arts and today's spiritual movement. Without equality of these three branches, truth, justice, and enlightenment are obscured and cannot be easily found.

Joy is one of the objectives in creating balance among the three voices of a society. Find joy in all you seek and do. The world is filled with chaos, anxiety, and fear but those are not of the spiritual world. The spiritual world blossoms with truth, wisdom, and love, which yields joy. When you are focused on truth, wisdom, and love there is no room for anxiety, fear, and chaos to enter.

Truth permeates the body, your thoughts, and heart. Where the light of truth resides, darkness cannot enter. Darkness gives birth to and nurtures the "I can't," the "what ifs," and the "why me" victimhood thinking. Victimhood is the acceptance of darkness in your world. Each of us can change the world for the better when we shut the door on darkness and turn toward truth and the light. There is a natural law of polarity with darkness and light; both are illumination, but only one serves humanity the best.

Truth speaks boldly with conviction and an empowered unrelenting compassion for the need for spiritual reconnection. In order to survive through the next decade people will need to put on a shield of truth. Truth leads to a spiritual connectedness to the Divine and the universe.

Truth is the Divine's word come to Earth. Truth is the Divine's sword to slay the evil dragons. Truth is mightier than the sword, but also acts like a sword. How do you survive when the world is disintegrating? You use your words to create the abundance and enlightenment you seek.

Truth is anything that is universally accepted as ancient fact or reality. Truth is something that must not be

The Sixth Principle: Truth

manipulated by cultural differences and political factions. TRUTH is the 6th Divine Way principle.

Once we accept truth as a universal principle, we can move forward, and one by one bring love and light to the world. It is universally accepted truth that is the glue that holds the planet, humanity, and the universe together. For example, if your lungs stopped working you wouldn't be able to breath on your own; you would lose consciousness and die. The truth in this case is that humans' lungs must work properly to maintain life. Or, should our planet Earth lose its gravitational pull, the energy that keeps us grounded, we and all matter like cars, trains, and planes would go rushing off into space, rain would no longer fall downward, and buildings would crumble. The truth here is that gravity is an energy field surrounding planet Earth and is necessary for humanity to live and survive.

In contrast, here is an example of something many people think of as truth, but in reality, it is not a universal truth because it is only true to a certain group of people. Each year a large portion of our population celebrates Easter. While Easter is a very important Christian holiday, it does not connect with any other major wisdom schools or lifestyle philosophies I studied. There are many such significant celebrations in the various forms of philosophies around the world, but because they have less coverage and are believed by millions of fewer people, they don't get much attention. Therefore, Easter would not be considered a universal principle but rather a principle of great importance specific to believers of Christianity. It is good to have a role model such as Jesus, but he never intended to become a replacement or stand-in for God, our Creator, the Divine Source.

Easter is a day to celebrate the resurrection of humanity—the connection of humanity to each other, to God, and to the universe, not just to idolize Jesus. So while Easter is a true story, it is not a truth principle.

Truth is not a commodity. When tampered with it becomes toxic, disruptive, and discriminatory—a weapon to control others. Truth must remain pure, crystal clear, and unadulterated for humanity and the universe to survive.

A society that is constantly fed half-truths is a society that cannot stand cohesively together and will crumble from within. It will be an easy target for seduction from within and destruction from without. False truths build contempt for others and breed hatred and unrest within the home and society. Universal truth is black and white; there are no gray areas like we've been fed for hundreds or thousands of years. Universal truth is found deep within the heart of a humanity burning brightly, while the darkness, fake truth, and bold lies lurk in the gray shadows.

The seven principles of this book, including TRUTH, will lead humanity back to a society that thrives—one that looks for the good in others and our commonalities. They will unify us as families, communities, and nations so we can live in a world filled with light and love. We will transform into a humanity that practices equality and justice for all and does not preach lies, prejudices, and hate.

Truth knows all wisdom and sees all truth in what is and isn't. Truth is the foundation of the universe and is also the foundation of humanity. Truth is the only way of living so peace, harmony, and joy can thrive on planet Earth. Truth is the alpha and omega of our planet; when truth thrives, chaos and fear subside. Truth unifies all, provides justice, and removes prejudice.

Many don't realize they are hungering, but they do know emptiness and the yearning for something, and that something is truth. Truth comes in many shapes and forms but is always recognizable because **truth improves all of humanity and does harm to no one**. Truth is found by being 100% connected to God and the universe 100% of the time.

A new way of life is exactly what the Divine Way is creating. This could be considered a new spiritual world order—not one that excludes religions, traditional worshipping, or rituals, but rather an all-inclusive way of life where the individual, humanity, planet Earth, and the universe co-exist and thrive.

Come Together in Truth

It is time to let go of the walls that separate us causing fear, chaos, and hatred. Walls that have divided:

- Parents vs children vs seniors
- Young vs old
- Race against race
- Country against country
- Humanity against the environment
- Humanity vs animals
- Adults against pre-born infants and children
- Haves vs have-nots
- Rich vs everyone else

It is these very walls that need to be torn down and new avenues of communication, connection, and co-existence created to flow through humanity. Think of it as a lifestyle change that encourages the world to find peace.

UNIVERSAL TRUTH #16
PEACE COMES FROM WITHIN.

Merging ancient wisdom with contemporary family life, diverse cultures, religions, ethics, and our truth within will yield a whole new lifestyle for our current reality—a way of life that will lead all of us to our fullest potential and to light, love, all that is, the Divine.

This new lifestyle must focus on compassion and commonality of humanity, and put little importance on the differences. All humans have a heart to feel, eyes to see, a brain to think, and blood that supplies oxygen and nutrients to the body while removing waste materials. Furthermore, the blood of all humanity bleeds red. We are the same just dressed in a different outer layer of skin, making everyone a beautiful individual creation of the Divine, the universe, the First Source.

We are all individuals yet belong to the same collective called humanity. As a member of the human race, we are one very small part of the whole. And when something happens to one of us, good or bad, the whole is affected. For example, in a family when a child is hurt at school, the whole family has compassion, feels the pain of the child, and sends the child good wishes and healing energy, even if the family doesn't understand this principle. If that same child is being honored for something, the whole family celebrates. When a child dies, all mothers feel the pain and grieve the loss of that child with that child's mother.

This important life philosophy of unity and connection is becoming a rapidly endangered way of life in our current reality. When positive energy-creating events bond families together, they stay connected, continue communicating, and raise the positive energy of our planet. When events like this do not happen, our energy levels are lowered and the family connection is devalued and disconnected.

Now, think of the family as a microcosm of our country, our planet. When our country is no longer a cohesive family, our values and guidelines for living are devalued and our country becomes broken because there is no truth. Then communication, compassion, and connection within our much larger family, the country, breaks down and we become isolated in desperate small groups.

This must stop! We need to reconnect, communicate, and belong to our larger community. If not, we will lose complete control. When we are no longer in control and no longer unified, someone else is!

Once we have lost connection and communication with each other on a local level, community level, and country level, we will lose everything, especially our freedom.

Generations of humanity have existed with a survival code energy system since the passing of ancient civilizations. This survival code is the basis for our current experiences, our beliefs, and our need of conformity. When survival is common ground or the foundation of a civilization, the only option seen by most is to conform. Conformity offers a form of protection that prevents individuals from standing out, independent thinking, and acting out of truth and wisdom. This predisposes that humanity must follow whatever they are told to survive. This is what we as humanity have been doing for millennia and what we are currently facing.

This is how we reached today's belief system. In order to survive you need to conform no matter what you are conforming to: clothing styles, celebrity beliefs, political decisions such as Hitler's in WWII, no matter how outrageous or who gets hurt.

The conformity code is yet another way for those in control to stay in control and keep all of us form seeking and speaking the truth. This thought process totally denies and obstructs the Divine way of the universe. A Divine way must be re-installed on planet Earth so love, light, and eternal enlightenment are the norm, not just scattered around the Earth like fireflies.

EMBRACE THE HEART-MIND CONNECTION

The conformity code is a mind-body system that needs to be converted to a heart-mind system where spirituality resides. The heart-mind system is where creativity, beauty, love, and light reside—where commonality and unity grow and harmony with nature returns. It is time for humanity to restructure their internal energy code and reach for the stars. When we are no longer hostages to conformity and survival but rather focused on

The Sixth Principle: Truth

creativity, joy, and an eternal connection to the All that is, we can thrive.

As the years and decades unfurl, humanity will discover an awareness of this new heart-mind code that will enable the shift from survival mode to the new heart-mind-spirit energy code manifesting the Divine Way of the universe. It will be filled with artistic expression, the sciences, creativity, and spirituality, all of which become rapidly integrated into daily lives. This is true enlightenment for humanity. This new code will have far reaching implications, both today and for generations of the next millennia.

Gone will be the survival-based self-interest of governments, businesses, religions, and sciences. All will be reformatted and a profound shift will take place. The access to this new heart-mind code can be found through meditation or a dream state. These altered states of consciousness provide a new energy that shifts and restructures the old. It's a transformation of the old into the new Divine Way.

The profound shifts produced by living the new Divine Way will help humanity become much less dependent upon the old survival and conformity code and integrate a unity code built upon creativity, commonality, and connection. The thread of truth will run through a new loop of spirituality, science, technology, music, and the arts. New ideas, insights, and innovation will flow into humanity to further expand a new connection, create a new renaissance, and upgrade the enlightenment of humanity.

This process will feed our new personal energy system with an enormous feeling of connection, belonging, support for each other, and the reality that we are close to finding our spiritual home. This connectedness feeling will run through us like a thread of love and a beam of light.

It is with great joy that millions of us around the world have taken steps on our journey to move enlightenment forward on humanity's path. The more enlightened humanity becomes, the less powerful those in control will be. The puppeteer will no long control what humanity does. The mass of puppets become those in control, bonded through commonality based on truth, not differences, a connection to each other and the Divine, while looking out for each other, the masses, not the villainous puppet masters.

The puppeteers will fight with every breath to prevent this major change in our world but will fail. Humanity has had enough and is looking to the future filled with peace, cooperation, connection, and the Divine Way.

Where there is compassion in the heart of humanity, love resides. When the heart is compassionless, control of others becomes the rule. Over the millennia, compassion for others has decreased, allowing a compassionless society to rise. "It's all about me" or "What's in it for me?" This is exactly where we find ourselves today—in a compassionless, selfish minority around the world trying to control the masses and become the majority.

As the masses are awakening spiritually by going within and finding truth, they are also awakening to the fact that their freedoms are being quietly eroded and dismantled piece by piece every day. These freedoms include things like personal health care choice, equal protection for all including innocent babies and seniors,

The Sixth Principle: Truth

speaking lies to minimize truth, safe travel through all neighborhoods and nations, government intrusion into personal lives, choice of religious worship, and prejudicial laws helping the entitled rather than the masses.

Having no compassion for others is closely linked to conformity. If you conform and have no compassion for the masses, you are welcomed by those trying to overrun and control the masses. If not, you are no longer welcome in their ivory towers of thought- police and re-education advocates trying to repress and indoctrinate the masses. Gone are free thinking and free speech. Only indoctrination of the masses by those in control is allowed.

LET THE TRUTH GROW

There is one more thing to consider when discussing truth: it expands. It grows in curious ways and at unexpected times. Once you know the truth you will realize very quickly that what is true today could change or morph into something larger and more expansive when you are at a point in your journey when you are ready to receive more information.

The truth itself, though, does not change. Again, it merely expands. For example, the moon looks like a beautiful silver ball with dimples when viewed from planet Earth. But what we've come to understand from various orbiting satellites and in person visits by astronauts is that those dimples are craters, and that there are rocks, dead volcanos, and lava flows that make up the moon. And it is not silver. The truth is that there is a moon, but through the centuries as we've learned more, it isn't a perfect smooth ball with a few dimples but instead has a rough textured surface with very low gravity, making visiting astronauts tumble over as they try to pick up soil samples.

Truth isn't linear; it is expansive like a spiral. What we knew to be the truth 200 years ago has vastly expanded. The truth will grow exponentially the more people seek the truth, oneness, and enlightenment.

It is time for light, love, and compassion to rise up in strength and numbers. Collectively we become one and make a stand against the tyranny of oppression, fear, and prejudice. The choice is clear: either we bow down to a new world form of slavery and hate or we rise up as a unified humanity built on love, truth, and wisdom.

It's time to become a world fueled by love and light. You are the light; we are the light. Anyone seeking a direct connection with our Creator, the One, the Divine, the First Source will quickly realize that darkness succeeds only if humanity buys into the fear, anger, and hatred put forth in darkness where it is often cloaked in half-truths and capitalizes on the pain and suffering of others

BEING ENOUGH FOR OUR SELF

Let's make it very clear that feelings are not evidence of truth or reality in that it is the clarity of awareness that we stand our worth upon. It is in the fact that we are divine essence in the form of spirit housed in this temple of the physical body, mind, and emotions. We understand we are dimensional, we claim our birth right, our birth awareness, and our birth duty to live in the reality that we are a divine essence in human form. No matter what the circumstance we find ourselves in that appears to be less than, if we are spiritually connected, we are enough for ourselves. The circumstance has no power over us.

The Sixth Principle: Truth

TRUTH matters!

Stand on your truth. Your truth is about creating heaven on Earth for you and humanity in this lifetime—first yours and then for others.

Be in the moment and you will find peace. Do not think and do not let your mind wander. Just breathe and be. Listen for the voice in your heart and see or hear the words appear. You just need to reach out, grasp it, and pull it in.

As a collective we are all facing the same darkness trying to overcome and control all. The dark side of the world thinks it has critical mass right now and can simply walk in and take over. They are so wrong and far from the truth.

ETERNAL CONNECTION

We will see the truth in everything that happens to us. And, because we can see the truth in everything that happens to us, we can do business and live our lives in a way that will help keep us from harm while ensuring prosperity.

Those who wish to control all for personal gain and hurt others in the process are the darkness. They think they have much power and control but when exposed to the truth and the light, their dark flame of hatred, anger, and deceit is revealed. Choose freedom from being tied down to the mundane. Lift your heart and let your soul soar like Jonathan Livingston Seagull. Don't believe the half-truths your eyes see and your ears hear. All they show is limitation. Look within your heart for understanding and clarity. Find out what you already know and you will see the way to fly.

When it comes to understanding and recognizing truth, practice discretion.

D	Do consider; believe only what your heart, not your brain, feels in truth.
I	Invest in time needed to believe or discard information.
S	Seek out alternative meanings for the information or alternative messages.
C	Consider all options of where the information came from, a prejudice of the messenger, etc., before making a decision.
R	Review! If it is significant information, take time to review it.
E	Every piece of information needs evaluating until you know it to be truth.
T	Treat all such information as sacred as you evaluate.
I	Invest time and work as necessary.
O	Own it if it is the truth.
N	No bad, inappropriate, or wrong ideas or thoughts are allowed.

Darkness thrives among the dark thinkers but cannot thrive in the light where it is exposed for what and who it is.

The division of humanity by those in control or trying to dominate us is the only way our unity can be destroyed. It is written into our DNA that humanity cannot be divided from each other, but that does not mean we don't have to work hard to protect it. The longer our

The Sixth Principle: Truth

thoughts and actions are bombarded with half-truths, the more difficult it becomes. We are one and must recognize each other at the heart level through unconditional love based on truth. Then and only then can unity take center stage.

> **Truth leads to Justice.**

Chapter 11
The Seventh Principle:
Love

Once you've experienced and have put into practice the first six Divine Way principles, number 7, LOVE will seem like a very natural transition to you. Why? Because you have done all the ground work, which automatically opens the door to infinite love, light, and oneness or consciousness.

The topic of oneness confuses many people. What do you believe about Oneness?

- Do you believe God, the One, the Divine is a separate being accessible only to those who use intermediaries deemed correct by various religions?
- Do you believe you can access the Divine when two or more are gathered together?

- Do you believe the Divine is an old, white-haired bearded entity that doesn't stop disease, chaos and death to humanity?

Most religions around the world hold and propagate these and other similar beliefs. The truth is, our Creator, the Divine, is none of the above but rather the Heart of the universe and all creation. Since this entity or being is neither male nor female, referring to the Heart of the universe as "he" or "she" is totally inappropriate. A better reference would simply be Love, Light, Spiritual Being, the Divine, or any of the other words used in this book to describe our Creator.

Oneness is the direct connection humanity shares with the Divine. It is an unbreakable bond or link that is never disconnected. You may not realize it, you may not know it, and you may not understand it, but **we have always been, are currently, and always will be connected** to the Divine and the Divine to us. We are one with the One.

We are the creator of our own little microcosm of the universe, but we are also part of the Whole and eternally connected to our Creator—the Creator of the entire universe. This connection is written into our DNA. Like a strand of gold spun thread, it is concealed deep within so those in control could never find nor alter it.

All paths lead to the Love, Light, Eternal Connection to Oneness. Oneness is the same place whether you grew up in a Far Eastern culture, the Middle East, Europe, Africa, Australia or the Americas ... whether you were in an Aboriginal tribe or a Native American tribe ... and whether you were from an Ancient Civilization or a

The Seventh Principle: Love

present one. All the paths to Oneness honor and show respect for the Heart of the universe, the Oneness of all.

Your journey isn't complete until you've reached an understanding about Oneness. This is a great dilemma for many, as it's easy to get confused by the information that many religions and cultures have put forth for thousands of years. Slightly or significantly different versions have been handed down through ancient wisdom.

The one thing most all agree upon is that there is a spiritual being or entity of thought that created everything and everyone. Some describe it as the Big Bang Theory, others as a creator God. But at the heart of everything lies the truth: there is a being or entity in the universe filled with love, energy, and light that is 100% connected to us eternally.

This connection will be denied, swept under a rug, beaten down by dictators, and tossed aside by deniers. It is truth you will find within because it was truth that was written within when humans were created. When you seek it, you will be shown the way and develop the will to find it. If you have already found it and want more, delve deeper into the truth within and you will find more. The truth grows as we grow.

The truth of oneness is expansive. What was true for us as children has expanded greatly over the years. The same thing happens when we journey further within. Truth blossoms, and with each new petal more is revealed. Just as the lotus flower grows in dirty, mucky water, as it blooms it reveals more and more truth and beauty with each petal. We too grow from the depths of darkness, chaos and fear and blossom in the light and love of our Creator.

It's like connecting the dots or playing electronic games. There is a natural progression, pathway, or flow of energy leading you. There are markers all along the way to let you know you are on the right path. Millions of others are somewhere on that same path with you. We are all on the journey together; some of us don't even know there is a journey and others are well ahead of us. It doesn't matter where you are or how fast you travel; what matters is that you are moving forward to a better life filled with peace, harmony, and prosperity based on truth and wisdom.

Some of us are leading the way and encouraging others to begin. Some of us are followers, grateful we have someone in front to guide us through the mountains and valleys of our journey. And of course, there will be those who are antagonistic to the massive change toward peace and prosperity that's taking place because they will lose control and their self-importance.

RECLAIM THE ULTIMATE CONNECTION

For the purpose of this book, I define Oneness as the coming together of humanity and the Great Spirit, the Creator, the First Source, the One, God, the Divine, or the Source. For thousands of years we've been taught that everything and everyone was separate—not only from each other and nature, but also from the First Source, the creator of the original thought and word that created the universe.

We, the collective we of humanity, have never been separate. Our hearts have always been merged whether with nature, animals, other humans, and the Divine, the ultimate Love and Light. It is written in our DNA. There

The Seventh Principle: Love

is no separateness. Life on planet Earth is connected life, a living, breathing, pulsating humanity. We either feel it and go with the energy flow of life, leading us to the completion of our journey back home to our eternal love, light and oneness, or we consume ourselves in false truths, disdain for others, and hatred of the masses.

You can experience this in societies everywhere. Those in control (the establishments, governments, and local leaders that look out for themselves) will exert power in whatever way possible to hold on to control—even if it means making decisions and taking actions that further control or jeopardize the lives and the future freedom of others.

While leadership requires tough decisions to be made, it also requires truth, equality, self-control, wisdom, respect, and honoring all as life in harmony with nature and a connected humanity. Taking all of this into consideration, a leader will embrace the value of all life and all paths to the six previous principles, which lead to the same place of love, light, and Oneness; a conscious humanity.

This is the way for humanity to live life to the fullest potential and to find inner peace. When you find Oneness, eternal love, and light, you eliminate issues created by cultures, race, religion, politics, corruption, fear, and victimology. When you find Oneness, you become transformed. Or, if you've already found Oneness, your transformation will be to a much deeper level when you apply the seven principles.

Humanity has been forced to live in survival mode for at least 2000 to 5000 years because of those in control: governments, the establishment, cultural beliefs and religions, and all the "ism" forced lifestyles. Millions of people have suffered persecution, savagery, and death all in the name of these controlling forces.

It is time to overcome all of these mechanisms of control, cultural conditioning, and all-encompassing servitude. It is time to move past ego, ours and everyone else's, and follow the path to love, light, and Oneness. Remember, **darkness cannot live in the light, hatred cannot live in love, and deceit cannot live where truth resides**. The conscious energy level of humanity must move rapidly toward love, light, and truth so peace and Oneness will become the rule of law for the planet, replacing hatred, intolerance, prejudice, and conflict. It is humanity's obligation to move the world into a new era of connection where peace resides.

A straight line may be the shortest distance between two points, but your line of connection with the One and the universe is even shorter. It is instant. It surpasses all that may stand in its way. Still your mind, find your heart center, and your connection is instantaneous. Touch your heart center to bring all your focus to that one spot where everything is instant. The knowing comes, the being is, and the love and light are eternal.

Reclaim Your Oneness

If the answers you seek about Oneness are still illusive, it is because you are trying to interpret it with your human mind. You are not alone. You are right to question how to express "I am one with the One." Some also say "I am the One," and believe that once you are one with the One, you are the One.

The Seventh Principle: Love

When I say "I am one with the One," it's like saying "I am one with God, First source, our Creator." It is totally different than saying "I am God" or "I am the Creator." While I am in charge of my life and what I create or manifest, I do not believe that I am the One. I am part of the One just as a raindrop or wave is part of the ocean. Together we are one.

When you address the issue of connection, humans have always been connected to the Creator. The Creator didn't disconnect from us thousands of civilizations ago; rather, humanity disconnected from the One, our Creator. We have always been one with the Creator. Now we are finally finding our way back home, so to say we are finally one with the One again is 100% accurate. We even share some of the same characteristics with the One, the Creator, the Divine. For example, we are free to speak, move about, listen to whatever we wish, and learn. Keeping in mind that all manifestation begins with a thought, we can create or manifest our own future through our freedom of creative choice. But it is not in our purview at this time to manifest a new solar system, a star, or a planet as a human.

It is in our purview however, to manifest our own heaven on Earth by living a life based on the seven ancient principles, the Divine Way, in this book. As we reconnect with our Creator and raise humanity's consciousness and light, darkness, hatred, and control by others will diminish.

UNIVERSAL TRUTH #17
DARKNESS CANNOT LIVE OR SHINE IN THE LIGHT!

It is important for humanity to understand that it must reach a critical mass of light, of oneness with each other, and transcend its self-imposed limitations along with the control by others to create a better world for all humanity. Then we can all become "the collective one" with the One regardless of race, religion, culture, ethnicity, or past self-limiting beliefs. That is when we will create our own long-time coming heaven on Earth.

As expounded upon earlier, love can overcome anything but not for those who have never seen or experienced it ... not for those who have the seeds of hatred sewn within by humans from the moment of birth ... not for those under oppressive rule or those with parents who do not implant and re-enforce right versus wrong, good versus evil, hope versus fear, and love versus hatred. These special people need the help of those already on their journey filled with love and light, who can show them compassion and lead by a loving example how to seek a better life. They need their hope reignited before they can move forward.

Choose living and love over existing. You are not here to exist but to find and give great joy, peace, and understanding to yourself and others.

Own the day. It is all yours. No one is standing in the way. Nothing is drawing you in opposite directions.

Own your day. Life is to be lived one day at a time and to be owned. Live in the present each day so you can catch a rainbow sweeping through the sky, read a book, paint a masterpiece, or write a best seller. Do whatever it takes to own a creative portion of each day. That is critical to your success.

No one created our playing field to be level and equal to all. But the playing field was designed to enable free will and real selection on the part of each individual life based on personal preference. Each one of us is an open book filled with unwritten pages ready for us to record universal truths and a way of life written into our DNA.

It is up to us as individuals to find ourselves. It is our will that awakens within and leads us to truth. It is our burning desire within that leads us to the last step: finding our eternal Oneness with our Creator, the One, the Great Spirit, Eternal Love, the Divine.

The Journey Ahead

We've been taught for centuries that there are only five senses: taste, touch, sight, hear, and smell. But as my research progressed it became obvious that there are at least two more senses: feeling and knowingness. I believe these last two have been recently awakened in humanity and become more valuable and profound the deeper you search within to become one with the One, the Divine. Your search for the invisible, Divine light, and love will make the love and light increasingly more visible for you, for me, and for all who seek.

The infinite vastness of the Divine, while invisible, also becomes unavoidable because nowhere and nothing exists without the Divine, the One. There is no such thing as the absence of the Divine anywhere in the universe. However, the Divine does not dictate where you journey or what your goals are. The Divine gave you freedom of choice. But the Divine is always with you. We, you and I, the Divine and you, the Divine and I are always connected in an eternal circle. Our Creator is the beginning of the circle, and when we travel on our journey and complete our circle, the Divine is also the end of our journey. That is our spiritual home.

Oneness, our connection with the Divine, always was, is, and will be eternal and infinite. It is time to end disbelief and replace it with a knowingness that the Divine is real and lives within each and every one of us. We are spiritual beings having a human experience waking up to realize our most important task in life is to find our way back home to our Creator, Love.

However, as we proceed on our journey, we are reminded that:

- All spiritual beings are equal; one is no better than the next.
- No one or nothing can be more divine than any other person or thing.
- Truth is truth only when conceptualized and put into words that apply equally to all and bring no harm to any.
- The answers you seek on your journey can be found only by going within, not through the mind.

The Seventh Principle: Love

- True freedom is any culture, society, or nation with the unobstructed access of one's choosing to the Divine, the One, the Creator.
- Peace, joy, love, beauty, light, and security dominate your spiritual being the closer you are to discovering your direct connection to the One.

When we walk through wind, rain, and storm we never walk alone. Within our heart it is written that we'll never walk alone. Within our human DNA strand is the blueprint for this eternal thread to the Divine, the One. It is the thread implanted within our:

- Spiritual being
- Insight
- Clarity on where we came from
- Implanted memory of our Creator
- The principles of eternity
- Right and wrong
- Values of the universe
- Wholeness

This thread or path laid out in your DNA strand never quits. It always flows … eternity always continues. Once you've reached this message deeply within, your insight, awareness, truth, and love will always flow and grow.

In our solar system we have our planet Earth, our moon, and the sun, which allows our planet and us to survive and thrive. Yes, there are other issues such as your distance from the sun, and moon, gravity etc., but it is the basics of three at play.

Looking Within

The universe is us. There is no them versus us, or the universe and God versus man. You are all one; we are all one; there are no separate parts. Your human experience is also that of a spiritual experience. What happens out there also happens within you, within me, and every human. **Out there is not some distant void but rather the macro of the micro within.**

It is all within, always has been and always will be. You are what your heart has always been, and your knowledge is that of the universe.

Reaching the knowledge within is your spiritual journey. There are several ways to do this and all of them include quieting your mind. Whether you use meditation, especially mindful meditation, journaling, painting, dream interpretation, quiet walks on the beach, or other forms of creativity, the only way to go deep within and reach a higher level of consciousness is to:

1. Get into a non-distracting quiet space.
2. Quiet your mind; close your eyes.
3. Focus; keep your mind free of thoughts or empty so new thoughts can enter.
4. Look and listen to see what is hiding behind the veil when you are in quiet solitude.
5. With closed eyes and an empty mind (quiet music for some), you will see and hear truth, love, and light.

Quiet your mind so you can hear. Close your eyes so you can see. Since you receive information through all your senses, they must be completely void of everything so you can bring the new information into your physical being. Keep a notebook nearby to write down your thoughts at the end of each session. Finding the Source is the end goal.

When you find your Creator, you have found love without boundaries—a love that is thought to be unattainable by most and recognized by almost all.

A good mantra would be:

"I am no longer a human body and mind in control of an eternal being. I am an eternal being in a human body (always have been, am, and always will be) in control of everything I see, touch, taste, smell, hear, create, learn, feel, and know".

Or, *"My Eternal Being is and always will be in control and my body and mind, and will do only those things my Eternal Being instructs. My Eternal Self is a perfect being in all ways (always has been, is, and always will be)."*

Eternal Access

When you access your heart,
You find your voice within
When you find your voice within,
You discover your path
When you travel down your path,
You become connected to God and the universe
Once you are connected to God and the universe
You find PEACE!

The knowledge within is power, but it follows the law of truth just as the stars follow the law in the universe. Words matter; words are important; they are how you

Looking Within

manifest. Fill yourself only with words that work for what you seek. If you wish to hear spiritual enlightenment, then fill your mind with words like "I am."

> I am delight.
> I am love.
> I am truth.
> I am peace.

Light, love, and connection are the answer to most questions on planet Earth. They embody the qualities of unconditional love, acceptance, forgiveness, understanding, and compassion for all life everywhere. Everything we seek, feel, or experience is a delicate balance of all three.

May we each find joy in our lives while we seek the truth.

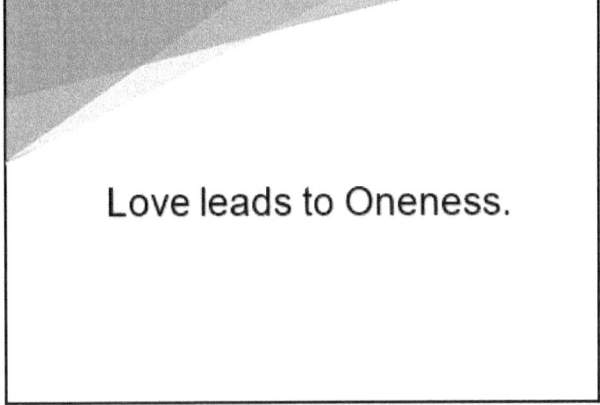

Bathed in the colors of the RAINBOW and energy of HOPE, PEACE, and JOY you EVOLVE. The cycle begins anew. The pattern of searching and growing continues as you merge into the New you. Every day you come closer to your WISHES and DREAMS.

Chapter 12
Adopting the Divine Way

One of the objectives of *Looking Within* is to shift energy on planet Earth. Together, we can derail evil so the positive energy on the planet can turn the corner and start its upward movement back to a new Golden Age. This is when feminine energy is in harmony with the masculine, and both are in harmony with nature. When the Divine Way is the primary lifestyle on Earth and with the return of music and the fine arts to culture, planet Earth and humanity can once again find balance and harmony.

Of course, there will be the obvious positive changes in our personal lives that result from having a direct connection with our Creator, the One, First Source, the Great Spirit. We will also finally know the truth planted deep within our DNA. But what are the macro benefits for humanity and planet Earth of using the seven principles of the Divine Way?

Would we be better off not changing anything, allowing the chaos to continue to grow and enslave all of us? Would we be better off allowing others to control us—people who look out only for their selfish self-interests? Would be we better off in a place where truth is no longer relevant and only prejudice, fear, hate, and injustice have a free reign?

What is happening on Earth today is only emblematic of things to come: freedoms being washed away and drowned in an ocean of pain; potential being cast into a hopeless dungeon of intolerance; hope being vanquished by gale force winds scattered into the four corners of the universe because of hate and discrimination. Is this the future we all hope for? NO! It is these very poisonous philosophies humanity needs to rid itself of. That is why the Divine Way must become the bridge to a new foundation for living our best lives now and overcoming millennia of subservience, inequality, and lies.

Just as there are seven principles, following them results in seven benefits to you, humanity, and the planet. Those benefits are:

Principle	Benefit
Wisdom	Enlightenment
Respect	Trust
Honor All	Harmony
Equality	Unity
Self-Control	Peace
Truth	Justice
Love	Oneness

Adopting the Divine Way

You might think we actually have all of the above benefits right now, but hold on—not so fast. You may think we have them because that's what we are told. However, universal truth shows that we have only bits and pieces based on half-truths. Consider this:

- When you have unity in the family and community, you have harmony in the nation.
- When you have harmony in the nation, freedom reigns.
- When freedom reigns across the lands, trust prevails everywhere.
- When trust is everywhere, justice rules.
- When justice rules, self-worth rises up from the ashes.
- When self-worth rises, there is peace in the world.

This is the simplest way to explain the long-term benefits of living your life the Divine Way. It is contagious like a smile; you can't get enough of it. Or it's like tossing a pebble into a pond. At first there's a splash, which creates a ripple. Then one ripple begets another and another and another, casting the message far and wide.

Once our self-worth is back to a healthy prosperous level, we can create the world we wish to live in: a world filled with Hope, Love, and Oneness that was envisioned by the Divine and recorded in ancient wisdom teachings. Remember:

- Without hope we cannot survive, but with hope we can create a better future.

- Without love we wither and die, but with love being eternal, infinite, and ever-present we thrive.
- Without joy there is nothing, but with joy comes a state of sustained wellbeing filled with happiness, peace within, and a knowingness that surpasses all understanding.

You have found your way home— a home where you can thrive in the physical world while being 100% connected 100% of the time in the spiritual world of the Divine.

Be the you who is connected, finds joy and peace within, and spreads it without. Be the person you came here to be, 100% connected to the Divine and the universe 100% of the time.

UNIVERSAL TRUTH #18
LIFE BEGINS WITH THE HOPE OF FINDING JOY.

Go within, far enough within, deep within, and you will find what you seek. The problem with society is we keep going further and further outside of self, seeking and finding more of what we already have, but it isn't enough. It is never enough.

CREATING TODAY

- Meditate daily. You will find peace.
- Read and re-read *Looking Within* until you find the truth.

Adopting the Divine Way

- Include creativity in your daily activities. Put it on your calendar. It reduces stress.
- Be yourself, 100% connected, confident, and in control. You will be empowered.
- Set the tone for the day when you arise. Begin the night before by setting your intent. You will accomplish more.
- See everything accomplished as you start your day. You will be more productive.
- Focus on something spiritual each day. Your connection will grow deeper.

If you feel empty, it's because you are not connected. When you are not connected, there is no or little joy in your life, no spiritual purpose in your life, no reason to get out of bed, no reason to care for yourself or others, and no reason to accomplish.

Light a candle and breathe. Center yourself so you can find your way home. Be you, the person you promised to be when you came to planet Earth as a baby. Be the you that is you, not the you everyone else thinks you should be.

Avoid the path that leads to darkness; it's where fear and hate reside. Change from a victimhood mindset filled with pain, discouragement, and disbelief to being in-control of yourself, filled with enthusiasm, joy, and inspiration. Go from confusion to clarity. "I am" is your inner being that is your authentic self. I am is enlightenment, Oneness. Remember, negative thoughts reduce your energy; positive thoughts increase your energy.

How do you connect with others when they think a connection is electronic, not at the soul level? You connect by using the 7 principles of the Divine Way.

The question needs to be asked, "Does what I have been doing get me closer to my spiritual goal, or does it distract me and take me further away from my goal of returning to God and the universe?" The more spiritual you become, the faster the information flows. To become more spiritual, you simply need to spend more time in silence. Today is the first day of the rest of your life. What are you going to do to make it worth the exchange for a day of your life? As you already know, if you do the most important thing first every day, everything else will fall into place. The Native American Creed says it beautifully.

The Creed

1. On the wings of eagle's soar,
    Set your goals on the universe above.
2. On the mighty buffalo be one,
    Connect Earth with the universe—be one.
3. On the backs of dolphin's swim,
    Everything is connected; water, land, the universe.
4. In the wolf's pack be at peace,
    When everyone is focused on the same goal everyone is safe and thrives.
5. In the wind, find stability,
    Wind is moving air and gives you life.

6. On the water, walk,
    Wherever you step you will be supported.
7. On the Earth, plant your seeds,
    The seeds you sow reveal you.
8. In the fire you will succeed,
    As the world worsens, you will bloom.

The Creed was the voice of millions of ancient souls that understood why they were here. They were here to experience the Earth, live on the Earth, and live in togetherness. Living as one with the Earth, living as one with each other, and living as one with the One. The Creed is their way and **the way**—the way they thought, acted, lived, and connected to all. No matter where they were, they lived it. It was when power and greed were introduced that the ancients became warriors needing to protect their own. And when they became divided within, they were overrun by others, conquered, and controlled.

Today, we are about staying connected 100% of the time; that's one way to describe it. Another way to describe it is to be a spiritually active listener. Either way works, but touches different hearts. Both take attention, focus, and time.

Take Time

Take time to breathe, you have much to do.
Take time to rest, you need to ration your energy.
Take time to be, you must live in the moment.
Take time to listen, the messages are always available.

Take time to reflect, you will tap into the eternal information.
Take time to connect, the universe awaits your arrival.
Take time to create, you will reach your destiny.
Take time to find joy, it makes your heart smile.
Take time to love yourself and others, you will find peace.

THE CHALLENGE

Follow the Divine Way's 7 principles for 21 days to transform your life and transcend all self-imposed limitations. When you do, you will find who you are, what you are eternally connected to, and your personal destiny. As a final reminder of what to focus on, here is the list of the 7 principles and the benefit of each. Before we end, take some time to fill in the last column, where you state what you commit to do in order to live each principle.

Adopting the Divine Way

Principle	Benefit	What I Commit to Doing
Wisdom	Enlightenment	
Respect	Trust	
Honor All	Harmony	
Equality	Unity	
Self-Control	Peace	
Truth	Justice	
Love	Oneness	

Remember that "You are," because you know the Divine and understand that you are one with the One. You are connected to the Divine, and the Divine is connected to you. You are part of the Divine's whole, and the Divine is part of your whole.

Be the you who contributes their share to the betterment of others, of society, and the universe. Be the you who gives more than they take and leaves humanity and Earth a better place than when you arrived. There is no fear of failure because your Creator, God, the One, the Divine is by your side. Failure is only one step on the road to success.

Epilogue
The Divine Way of the Universe

Evil is alive and well. Life is very hard to live when evil prevails. The constant chaos keeps everyone on edge and worried. It gives evil leaders strength to control others and destroy those who won't follow. You see it everywhere in society today, much as earlier generations saw it with Hitler, Mussolini, and Stalin.

When your day begins, so does your life journey move forward. When 100% connected to the Divine, you are receiving information; the information is always flowing and you are understanding it.

The journey is long and difficult for some; for others it takes place in the blink of an eye. It is the journey and finding our way back home that matters. We are no longer lost sheep or a family divided. We are one humanity treating each other with dignity and respect, honoring the land and its resources for generations to come, and being 100% connected to our Creator, the Divine.

Looking Within

There is no greater blessing in the world than to know we are at peace, on the inside and the outside. This is the kind of peace that passes all understanding. We have created our own heaven on Earth.

This process may take several decades or maybe a couple of centuries to fully bloom around the world, but bloom it will. Once the seeds of enlightenment are sewn, they will sprout wherever they land and no controlling interests will be able to stop the tsunami of enlightenment that will blanket the Earth. Enlightenment will sprout in cement cities, will overcome noise pollution, and will seep into every crevice and every hardened heart. It will flow like molten lava, the Blue Danube, the Nile, the Amazon, and the Mississippi rivers creating its own path for generations to come.

The mountains will bow in homage to the waves from the ocean of humanity, and the new Renaissance of Joy will fall on the Earth. It will be like a blanket of soft pure white snow so that all may see, hear, feel, touch, taste, and sense that a new and vastly upgraded era of civility, peace, and joy have overcome all the hate, lies, deceit, and control by others for millennia to come.

Rest in knowing that hope, peace, and joy reside within and without when joy rules the world.

Epilogue: The Divine Way of the Universe

Begin Each Day

Begin every day with a smile.
You will set a happier tone for the day.
Begin every day with a grateful heart,
Gratitude is the key to attracting a better future.
Begin every day by organizing your thoughts,
You will focus on the important, not the urgent.
Begin every day with positive thoughts,
They will increase your energy.
Begin every day by putting on clothes that energize your intent,
You will be in control of your energy all day.
Begin every day by making your bed,
You have successfully completed your first project and have turned chaos into order.
Begin every day by reviewing your intent from the night before,
Arrange them into doable tasks, you will accomplish more.
Begin every day as if it could be your last,
You will be at peace and have no regrets.

Life changes constantly. Sometimes we are moving up a hill, other times sideways, and occasionally backwards, but life is always moving and changing. That's okay. It is much like the ebb and flow of waves. Waves can be gently lapping the shore or those same waves can be ferocious and deadly during a storm.

It's up to us to choose whether we are going to let the hostile storms of life crush and defeat us, or if we are going to take control and turn the ferocious deadly waves of life into calm and peaceful waves, gently kissing the shores of our life. It's up to us.

Do You Know

Do you know, it is your turn
Do you know, it is your turn to unveil you
Do you know, you are connected
Do you know, the universe and others await
Do you know, you are important because you are you?

The choice is yours. The choice is ours. Boldly create the future you want so you can thrive, so we can thrive, and so we (humanity) can find peace and confidently live a life full of hope, peace, love, and joy.

This message is the right message for humanity in need. It is an investment into the future of humanity, which dares to change and meet its destiny. Together, we will bravely rise up and transform humanity to meet and surpass the demands of an ever-changing future … Together, we will usher in the Renaissance of Joy.

Glossary

As above so below: What happens in the heavens above (meaning the stars and planets commonly referred to as the study of astrology), happens below. It matters when and where you are born, because there is no one else exactly like you.

Astrology: The roadmap of your destiny written in the stars.

Consciousness: An awareness that we have a higher self, a knowing that I AM.

Enlightenment: 100% connection 100% of the time with our Creator, the Divine, and balance in all thing and energies.

Era of Connection: A knowingness that all things, humanity, the planet, and universe are always connected to the Divine.

Manifestation: What happens when you create through a thought and place your focus and energy on what you desire; where you place your focus and energy becomes your reality.

Metaphysical: The interaction of all that is.

Oneness: The coming together of humanity with each other and the Creator, the One, God, the Divine.

Renaissance of Joy: A revival of the arts, music, and creativity as an integral component of daily life and the new found joy on Earth.

Religion: Specific beliefs and life philosophies around the world.

Spirituality: The increasing awareness of a higher consciousness, an uninterrupted connection with the Divine life-giving energy force and the universe.

Transformation: Taking something ordinary or old and turning it into something better or extraordinary.

Truth: When conceptualized and put into words, it applies equally to all and brings no harm to any.

Wisdom: Having knowledge and judgment and using it appropriately to improve self, others and bring no harm to anyone.

Universal Truths

Chapter 1
UNIVERSAL TRUTH #1: You are a spiritual being 100% connected to God and the Universe 100% of the time.

UNIVERSAL TRUTH #2: Humanity is always connected to each other, God, and the Universe.

Chapter 2
UNIVERSAL TRUTH #3: We can do what we want if it is in our best interest, in the interest of those surrounding us, **and brings no harm to others.**

UNIVERSAL TRUTH #4; Humans are divine beings having a human experience, not humans seeking a divine experience.

UNIVERSAL TRUTH #5: Humanity is diversity unified as the human race.

Chapter 3
UNIVERSAL TRUTH #6: Silence is the foundation for spiritual connection.

Chapter 4
UNIVERSAL TRUTH #7: Change is the only guaranteed constant in our lives.

Chapter 5

UNIVERSAL TRUTH #8: Wisdom is knowing the truth and applying it to all you think, say, feel, and do.

Chapter 6

UNIVERSAL TRUTH #9: All human life is precious and a gift from God.

UNIVERSAL TRUTH #10: Treat others as you wish to be treated.

UNIVERSAL TRUTH #11: To be a conscious creator you need to always be in control of your own thoughts.

UNIVERSAL TRUTH #12: What you focus on becomes your reality. Your existing reality is what you've focused on in the past.

Chapter 7

UNIVERSAL TRUTH #13: Planet Earth had perfect balance, harmony, hope, peace, and joy when it was created.

Chapter 8

UNIVERSAL TRUTH #14: Connecting within helps create better life experiences and provides you direction.

Chapter 9

UNIVERSAL TRUTH #15: Everything you think, say, feel, and do matters because that is how you create your future.

Chapter 10
UNVERSAL TRUTH #16: Peace comes from within.

Chapter 11
UNIVERSAL TRUTH #17: Darkness cannot live or shine in the light!

Chapter 12
UNIVERSAL TRUTH #18: Life begins with the hope of finding joy.

About the Author

Pat Heydlauff is an expert at designing home and workplace environments that reduce stress, improve work/life balance, increase prosperity, and build knowledge in Feng Shui principles. She provides people with a roadmap that's crucial for navigating through today's chaos, technological interruptions, and financial dictates. Through the 7 Divine Principles from *Looking Within*, she helps people open their hearts so they can see the truth, open their ears to hear the Divine's whispers, and open their thinking so they can love, flourish, and connect.

Known as "The Renaissance Woman" Pat is a Flow of Focus Strategist; Work/Life Balance, Prosperity, and WorkForce Expert; and Feng Shui Expert. She is certified in Organization Management, Neuro Linguistic Programming, and Time Line Therapy. She is also the founder of the groundbreaking "Flow of Focus" System for Leadership & Efficiency.

Pat's mission is to help individuals unlock their full potential to live a truly stress-free, prosperous, and meaningful life, and to guide businesses to a path of maximum productivity, profitability, and efficiency.

Contact her at www.PatHeydlauff.com.

www.ingramcontent.com/pod-product-compliance
Lightning Source LLC
Chambersburg PA
CBHW070423010526
44118CB00014B/1874